THE CATHEDRAL AND THE BAZAAR

*Musings on Linux and Open Source by an
Accidental Revolutionary*

THE CATHEDRAL AND THE BAZAAR

*Musings on Linux and Open Source by an
Accidental Revolutionary*

ERIC S. RAYMOND

with a foreword by Bob Young

BEIJING · CAMBRIDGE · FARNHAM · KÖLN · SEBASTOPOL · TOKYO

*The Cathedral and the Bazaar: Musings on Linux and
Open Source by an Accidental Revolutionary, Revised Edition*
by Eric S. Raymond

Copyright © 1999, 2001 by Eric S. Raymond.
Printed in the United States of America.

Published by O'Reilly Media, Inc., 1005 Gravenstein Highway North,
Sebastopol, CA 95472.

Editor: Tim O'Reilly

Production Editor: Sarah Jane Shangraw

Cover Art Director/Designer: Edie Freedman

Interior Designers: Edie Freedman, David Futato, and Melanie Wang

Printing History:

October 1999:	First Edition
January 2001:	Revised Edition

Library of Congress Cataloging-in-Publication data is available at:
http://www.oreilly.com/catalog/cathbazpaper/.

ISBN: 978-0-596-00108-7
[LSI]

[2011-06-10]

TO THE MEMORY OF ROBERT ANSON HEINLEIN

For the many lessons he taught me:
to respect competence, to value and defend freedom,
and especially, that specialization is for insects.

✦ ✦ ✦

TABLE OF CONTENTS

FOREWORD

✦ ✦ ✦

Freedom is not an abstract concept in business.

The success of any industry is almost directly related to the degree of freedom the suppliers and the customers of that industry enjoy. Just compare the innovation in the U.S. telephone business since AT&T lost its monopoly control over American consumers with the previously slow pace of innovation when those customers had no freedom to choose.

The world's best example of the benefits of freedom in business is a comparison of the computer hardware business and the computer software business. In computer hardware, where freedom reigns for both suppliers and consumers alike on a global scale, the industry generates the fastest innovation in product and customer value the world has ever seen. In the computer software industry, on the other hand, change is measured in decades. The office suite, the 1980s killer application, wasn't challenged until the 1990s with the introduction of the web browser and server.

Open-source software brings to the computer software industry even greater freedom than the hardware manufacturers and consumers have enjoyed.

Computer languages are called languages because they are just that. They enable the educated members of our society (in this case, programmers) to build and communicate ideas that benefit the other members of our society, including other programmers. Legally restricting access to knowledge of the infrastructure that our society increasingly relies on (via the proprietary binary-only software licenses our industry historically has used) results in less freedom and slower innovation.

Open source represents some revolutionary concepts being thrown at an industry that thought it had all of its fundamental structures worked out. It gives customers control over the technologies they use, instead of enabling the vendors to control their customers through restricting access to the code behind the technologies. Supplying open-source tools to the market will require new business models. But by delivering unique benefits to the market, those companies that develop the business models will be very successful competing with companies that attempt to retain control over their customers.

There have always been two things that would be required if open-source software was to materially change the world: one was for open-source software to become widely used and the other was that the benefits this software development model supplied to its users had to be communicated and understood.

This is Eric Raymond's great contribution to the success of the open-source software revolution, to the adoption of Linux-based operating systems, and to the success of open-source users and the companies that supply them. Eric's ability to explain clearly, effectively, and accurately the benefits of this revolutionary software development model has been central to the success of this revolution.

—*Bob Young, Chairman and CEO, Red Hat, Inc.*

PREFACE: WHY YOU SHOULD CARE

✦ ✦ ✦

The book in your hands is about the behavior and culture of computer hackers. It collects a series of essays originally meant for programmers and technical managers. The obvious (and entirely fair) question for you, the potential reader, to ask is: "Why should I care?"

The most obvious answer to this question is that computer software is an increasingly critical factor in the world economy and in the strategic calculations of businesses. That you have opened this book at all means you are almost certainly familiar with many of today's truisms about the information economy, the digital age, and the wired world; I will not rehearse them here. I will simply point out that any significant advance in our understanding of how to build better-quality, more reliable software has tremendous implications that are growing more tremendous by the day.

The essays in this book did not invent such a fundamental advance, but they do describe one: open-source software, the process of systematically harnessing open development and decentralized peer review to lower costs and improve software quality. Open-source software is not a new idea (its traditions go back to the beginnings of the Internet thirty years ago), but only recently have technical and market forces converged to draw it out of a niche role. Today the open-source movement is bidding strongly to define the computing infrastructure of the next century. For anyone who relies on computers, that makes it an important thing to understand.

I just referred to the "open-source movement". That hints at other and perhaps more ultimately interesting reasons for the reader to care. The idea of open source has been pursued, realized, and cherished over those thirty years by a vigorous tribe of partisans native to the Internet. These are the people who proudly call themselves "hackers"—not as the term is now abused by journalists to mean a computer criminal, but in its true and original sense of an enthusiast, an artist, a tinkerer, a problem solver, an expert.

The tribe of hackers, after decades spent in obscurity struggling against hard technical problems and the far greater weight of mainstream indifference and dismissal, has recently begun to come into its own. They built the Internet; they built Unix; they built the World Wide Web; they're building Linux and open-source software today; and, following the great Internet explosion of the mid-1990s, the rest of the world is finally figuring out that it should have been paying more attention to them all along.

The hacker culture and its successes pose by example some fundamental questions about human motivation, the organization of work, the future of professionalism, and the shape of the firm—and about how all of these things will change and evolve in the information-rich post-scarcity economies of the 21st century and beyond. The hacker culture also, arguably, prefigures some profound changes in the way humans will relate to and reshape their economic surroundings. This should make what we know about the hacker culture of interest to anyone else who will have to live and work in the future.

This book is a collection of essays that were originally published on the Internet; *A Brief History of Hackerdom* is originally from 1992, but has since been regularly updated and revised, and the others were written between February 1997 and May 1999. They were somewhat revised and expanded for the first edition in

October 1999, and updated again for this second edition of January 2001, but no really concerted attempt has been made to remove technicalia or make them more accessible (e.g., dumb them down) for a general audience. I think it more respectful to puzzle and challenge an audience than to bore and insult it. If you have difficulty with particular technical or historical points or the odd computer acronym, feel free to skip ahead; the whole does tell a story, and you may find that what you learn later makes sense of what puzzled you earlier.

The reader should also understand that these essays are evolving documents, into which I periodically merge the distilled results of feedback from people who write to comment on or correct them. While I alone remain responsible for any errors in this book, it has benefitted from a peer-review process very like that which it describes for software, and incorporates contributions from people too numerous to list here. The versions printed here are not fixed or final forms; rather, they should be considered reports from a continuing inquiry in which many members of the culture they describe are active participants.

Finally, I must at least try to express my delight and amazement and gratitude for the many people and the long chain of apparently fortuitous circumstances that have led up to this book . . . .

Some particular thanks are due for long-term friendship and support for the work captured between these covers. Thank you, Linus Torvalds. Thank you, Larry Augustin. Thank you, Doc Searls. Thank you, Tim O'Reilly. You are all people I am proud to call friends as well as colleagues. Most especially: thank you, Catherine Raymond — my love, my wife, and my longest-time supporter.

I am a hacker. I have been part of the culture described in this book for more than 20 years. In that time I have been privileged to work and play with some of the most interesting and exceptional people on Earth, solving fascinating problems and (on a precious few occasions) creating something both genuinely new and useful. Too many of those people to name here have taught me valuable lessons, about our shared craft and many other things. The essays in this book are my return gift to them.

These essays were stages of discovery for me as well, reports from a fascinating journey in which I learned to see the long-familiar in a new and deeper way. To my then and continuing astonishment, the mere act of reporting this journey turned out to have a catalyzing effect on the emergence of open source into the mainstream. I hope the reader of my travel papers will catch some of the excitement of that journey and of the amazing prospects that are unfolding before us today as mainstream business and consumers take their first steps on the same road.

Revision Notes for the Second Edition

For the benefit of readers of the first edition, here follows a summary of topics on which there have been substantive additions or revisions in the second edition:

How many eyeballs tames complexity. The deadliness of deadlines. A more precise definition of forking and pseudoforking. The relevance of evolutionary handicap theory, peacocks, and stags to open-source developer motivation. Economically, why isn't open source underprovided? Effects of asymmetric information. Open-sourcing as a competitive weapon. The predictions in *Revenge of the Hackers* have been examined from the perspective of one year later, and new ones added. An appendix on the growth of the fetchmail project has been added.

A BRIEF HISTORY OF HACKERDOM

✦ ✦ ✦

I explore the origins of the hacker culture, including pre-history among the Real Programmers, the glory days of the MIT hackers, and how the early ARPAnet nurtured the first network nation. I describe the early rise and eventual stagnation of Unix, the new hope from Finland, and how "the last true hacker" became the next generation's patriarch. I sketch the way Linux and the mainstreaming of the Internet brought the hacker culture from the fringes of public consciousness to its current prominence.

Prologue: The Real Programmers

In the beginning, there were Real Programmers.

That's not what they called themselves. They didn't call themselves hackers, either, or anything in particular; the sobriquet 'Real Programmer' wasn't coined until after 1980, retrospectively by one of their own. But from 1945 onward, the technology of computing attracted many of the world's brightest and most creative minds. From Eckert and Mauchly's first ENIAC computer onward there was a more or less continuous and self-conscious technical culture of enthusiast programmers, people who built and played with software for fun.

The Real Programmers typically came out of engineering or physics backgrounds. They were often amateur-radio hobbyists. They wore white socks and polyester shirts and ties and thick glasses and coded in machine language and assembler and FOR-TRAN and half a dozen ancient languages now forgotten.

From the end of World War II to the early 1970s, in the great days of batch processing and the "big iron" mainframes, the Real Programmers were the dominant technical culture in computing. A few pieces of revered hacker folklore date from this era, including various lists of Murphy's Laws and the mock-German "Blinkenlights" poster that still graces many computer rooms.

Some people who grew up in the Real Programmer culture remained active into the 1990s. Seymour Cray, designer of the Cray line of supercomputers, was among the greatest. He is said to have once toggled an entire operating system of his own design into a computer of his own design through its front-panel switches. In octal. Without an error. And it worked. Real Programmer macho supremo.

The 'Real Programmer' culture, though, was heavily associated with batch (and especially batch scientific) computing. It was eventually eclipsed by the rise of interactive computing, the universities, and the networks. These gave birth to another engineering tradition that, eventually, would evolve into today's open-source hacker culture.

THE EARLY HACKERS

The beginnings of the hacker culture as we know it today can be conveniently dated to 1961, the year MIT acquired the first PDP-1. The Signals and Power Committee of MIT's Tech Model Railroad Club adopted the machine as their favorite tech-toy and invented programming tools, slang, and an entire surrounding culture that is still recognizably with us today. These early years have been examined in the first part of Steven Levy's book *Hackers*, Anchor/Doubleday 1984, ISBN 0-385-19195-2.

MIT's computer culture seems to have been the first to adopt the term 'hacker'. The Tech Model Railroad Club's hackers became the nucleus of MIT's Artificial Intelligence Laboratory, the world's leading center of AI research into the early 1980s. Their influence was spread far wider after 1969, the first year of the ARPAnet.

The ARPAnet was the first transcontinental, high-speed computer network. It was built by the Defense Department as an experiment in digital communications, but grew to link together hundreds of universities and defense contractors and research laboratories. It enabled researchers everywhere to exchange information with unprecedented speed and flexibility, giving a huge boost to collaborative work and tremendously increasing both the pace and intensity of technological advance.

But the ARPAnet did something else as well. Its electronic highways brought together hackers all over the U.S. in a critical mass;

instead of remaining in isolated small groups each developing their own ephemeral local cultures, they discovered (or re-invented) themselves as a networked tribe.

The first intentional artifacts of the hacker culture—the first slang lists, the first satires, the first self-conscious discussions of the hacker ethic—all propagated on the ARPAnet in its early years. In particular, the first version of the Jargon File (*http://www.tuxedo.org/jargon*) developed as a cross-net collaboration during 1973–1975. This slang dictionary became one of the culture's defining documents. It was eventually published as *The Hacker's Dictionary* in 1983; that first version is out of print, but a revised and expanded version is *The New Hacker's Dictionary*, MIT Press, 3rd edition 1996, ISBN 0-262-68092-0 .

Hackerdom flowered at the universities connected to the net, especially (though not exclusively) in their computer science departments. MIT's AI and LCS labs made it first among equals from the late 1960s. But Stanford University's Artificial Intelligence Laboratory (SAIL) and Carnegie-Mellon University (CMU) became nearly as important. All were thriving centers of computer science and AI research. All attracted bright people who contributed great things to the hacker culture, on both the technical and folkloric levels.

To understand what came later, though, we need to take another look at the computers themselves, because the AI Lab's rise and its eventual fall were both driven by waves of change in computing technology.

Since the days of the PDP-1, hackerdom's fortunes had been woven together with Digital Equipment Corporation's PDP series of minicomputers. DEC pioneered commercial interactive computing and time-sharing operating systems. Because their machines were flexible, powerful, and relatively cheap for the era, lots of universities bought them.

Cheap time-sharing was the medium the hacker culture grew in, and for most of its lifespan the ARPAnet was primarily a network of DEC machines. The most important of these was the PDP-10, first released in 1967. The 10 remained hackerdom's favorite machine for almost fifteen years; TOPS-10 (DEC's operating system for the machine) and MACRO-10 (its assembler) are still remembered with nostalgic fondness in a great deal of slang and folklore.

MIT, though it used the same PDP-10s as everyone else, took a slightly different path; it rejected DEC's software for the PDP-10 entirely and built its own operating system, the fabled ITS.

ITS stood for "Incompatible Time-sharing System" which gives one a pretty good fix on the MIT hackers' attitude. They wanted it *their* way. Fortunately for all, MIT's people had the intelligence to match their arrogance. ITS, quirky and eccentric and occasionally buggy though it always was, hosted a brilliant series of technical innovations and still arguably holds the record as the single time-sharing system in longest continuous use.

ITS itself was written in assembler, but many ITS projects were written in the AI language LISP. LISP was far more powerful and flexible than any other language of its day; in fact, it is still a better design than most languages of *today*, 25 years later. LISP freed ITS's hackers to think in unusual and creative ways. It was a major factor in their successes, and remains one of hackerdom's favorite languages.

Many of the ITS culture's technical creations are still alive today; the EMACS program editor is perhaps the best-known. And much of ITS's folklore is still 'live' to hackers, as one can see in the Jargon File (*http://www.tuxedo.org/jargon*).

SAIL and CMU weren't asleep, either. Many of the cadre of hackers that grew up around SAIL's PDP-10 later became key figures in the development of the personal computer and today's window/icon/mouse software interfaces. Meanwhile hackers at CMU were doing the work that would lead to the first practical large-scale applications of expert systems and industrial robotics.

Another important node of the culture was XEROX PARC, the famed Palo Alto Research Center. For more than a decade, from the early 1970s into the mid-1980s, PARC yielded an astonishing volume of groundbreaking hardware and software innovations. The modern mice, windows, and icons style of software interface was invented there. So were the laser printer and the local-area network; and PARC's series of D machines anticipated the powerful personal computers of the 1980s by a decade. Sadly, these prophets were without honor in their own company; so much so that it became a standard joke to describe PARC as a place characterized by developing brilliant ideas for everyone else. Their influence on hackerdom was pervasive.

The ARPAnet and the PDP-10 cultures grew in strength and variety throughout the 1970s. The facilities for electronic mailing lists that had been used to foster cooperation among continent-wide special-interest groups were increasingly also used for more social and recreational purposes. DARPA deliberately turned a blind eye to all the technically 'unauthorized' activity; it understood that the extra overhead was a small price to pay for attracting an entire generation of bright young people into the computing field.

Perhaps the best-known of the 'social' ARPAnet mailing lists was the SF-LOVERS list for science-fiction fans; it is still very much alive today, in fact, on the larger 'Internet' that ARPAnet evolved into. But there were many others, pioneering a style of communication that would later be commercialized by for-profit time-sharing services like CompuServe, GEnie, and Prodigy (and later still dominated by AOL).

Your historian first became involved with the hacker culture in 1977 through the early ARPAnet and science-fiction fandom. From then onward, I personally witnessed and participated in many of the changes described here.

THE RISE OF UNIX

Far from the bright lights of the ARPAnet, off in the wilds of New Jersey, something else had been going on since 1969 that would eventually overshadow the PDP-10 tradition. The year of ARPAnet's birth was also the year that a Bell Labs hacker named Ken Thompson invented Unix.

Thompson had been involved with the development work on a time-sharing OS called Multics, which shared common ancestry with ITS. Multics was a test-bed for some important ideas about how the complexity of an operating system could be hidden inside it, invisible to the user, and even to most programmers. The idea was to make using Multics from the outside (and programming for it!) much simpler, so that more real work could get done.

Bell Labs pulled out of the project when Multics displayed signs of bloating into an unusable white elephant (the system was later marketed commercially by Honeywell but never became a success). Ken Thompson missed the Multics environment, and began to play at implementing a mixture of its ideas and some of his own on a scavenged DEC PDP-7.

Another hacker named Dennis Ritchie invented a new language called C for use under Thompson's embryonic Unix. Like Unix, C was designed to be pleasant, unconstraining, and flexible. Interest in these tools spread at Bell Labs, and they got a boost in 1971 when Thompson and Ritchie won a bid to produce what we'd now call an office automation system for internal use there. But Thompson & Ritchie had their eye on a bigger prize.

Traditionally, operating systems had been written in tight assembler to extract the absolute highest efficiency possible out of their host machines. Thompson and Ritchie were among the first to realize that hardware and compiler technology had become good enough that an entire operating system could be written in C, and by 1978 the whole environment had been successfully ported to several machines of different types.

This had never been done before, and the implications were enormous. If Unix could present the same face, the same capabilities, on machines of many different types, it could serve as a common software environment for all of them. No longer would users have to pay for complete new designs of software every time a machine went obsolete. Hackers could carry around software toolkits between different machines, rather than having to re-invent the equivalents of fire and the wheel every time.

Besides portability, Unix and C had some other important strengths. Both were constructed from a "Keep It Simple, Stupid" philosophy. A programmer could easily hold the entire logical structure of C in his head (unlike most other languages before or since) rather than needing to refer constantly to manuals; and Unix was structured as a flexible toolkit of simple programs designed to combine with each other in useful ways.

The combination proved to be adaptable to a very wide range of computing tasks, including many completely unanticipated by the designers. It spread very rapidly within AT&T, in spite of the lack of any formal support program for it. By 1980 it had spread to a large number of university and research computing sites, and thousands of hackers considered it home.

The workhorse machines of the early Unix culture were the PDP-11 and its descendant, the VAX. But because of Unix's portability, it ran essentially unaltered on a wider range of machines than one could find on the entire ARPAnet. And nobody used assembler; C programs were readily portable among all these machines.

Unix even had its own networking, of sorts—UUCP: low-speed and unreliable, but cheap. Any two Unix machines could exchange point-to-point electronic mail over ordinary phone lines; this capability was built into the system, not an optional extra. In 1980 the first Usenet sites began exchanging broadcast news, forming a gigantic distributed bulletin board that would quickly grow bigger than ARPAnet. Unix sites began to form a network nation of their own around Usenet.

A few Unix sites were on the ARPAnet themselves. The PDP-10 and Unix/Usenet cultures began to meet and mingle at the edges, but they didn't mix very well at first. The PDP-10 hackers tended to consider the Unix crowd a bunch of upstarts, using tools that looked ridiculously primitive when set against the baroque, lovely complexities of LISP and ITS. "Stone knives and bearskins!" they muttered.

And there was yet a third current flowing. The first personal computer had been marketed in 1975; Apple was founded in 1977, and advances came with almost unbelievable rapidity in the years that followed. The potential of microcomputers was clear, and attracted yet another generation of bright young hackers. *Their* language was BASIC, so primitive that PDP-10 partisans and Unix aficionados both considered it beneath contempt.

THE END OF ELDER DAYS

So matters stood in 1980: three cultures, overlapping at the edges but clustered around very different technologies. The ARPAnet/PDP-10 culture, wedded to LISP and MACRO and TOPS-10 and ITS and SAIL. The Unix and C crowd with their PDP-11s and VAXen and pokey telephone connections. And an anarchic horde of early microcomputer enthusiasts bent on taking computer power to the people.

Among these, the ITS culture could still claim pride of place. But stormclouds were gathering over the Lab. The PDP-10 technology ITS depended on was aging, and the Lab itself was split into factions by the first attempts to commercialize artificial intelligence. Some of the Lab's (and SAIL's and CMU's) best were lured away to high-paying jobs at startup companies.

The death blow came in 1983, when DEC cancelled its Jupiter follow-on to the PDP-10 in order to concentrate on the PDP-11 and

VAX lines. ITS no longer had a future. Because it wasn't portable, it was more effort than anyone could afford to move ITS to new hardware. The Berkeley variant of Unix running on a VAX became the hacking system *par excellence*, and anyone with an eye on the future could see that microcomputers were growing in power so rapidly that they were likely to sweep all before them.

It's around this time that Levy wrote *Hackers*. One of his prime informants was Richard M. Stallman (inventor of Emacs), a leading figure at the Lab and its most fanatical holdout against the commercialization of Lab technology.

Stallman (who is usually known by his initials and login name, RMS) went on to form the Free Software Foundation and dedicate himself to producing high-quality free software. Levy eulogized him as "the last true hacker", a description which happily proved incorrect.

Stallman's grandest scheme neatly epitomized the transition hackerdom underwent in the early eighties—in 1982 he began the construction of an entire clone of Unix, written in C and available for free. His project was known as the GNU (Gnu's Not Unix) operating system, in a kind of recursive acronym. GNU quickly became a major focus for hacker activity. Thus, the spirit and tradition of ITS was preserved as an important part of the newer, Unix and VAX-centered hacker culture.

Indeed, for more than a decade after its founding RMS's Free Software Foundation would largely define the public ideology of the hacker culture, and Stallman himself would be the only credible claimant to leadership of the tribe.

It was also around 1982–83 that microchip and local-area network technology began to have a serious impact on hackerdom. Ethernet and the Motorola 68000 microchip made a potentially potent combination, and several different startups had been formed to build the first generation of what we now call workstations.

In 1982, a group of Unix hackers from Stanford and Berkeley founded Sun Microsystems on the belief that Unix running on relatively inexpensive 68000-based hardware would prove a winning combination for a wide variety of applications. They were right, and their vision set the pattern for an entire industry. While still priced out of reach of most individuals, workstations were cheap for corporations and universities; networks of them (one to a user) rapidly replaced the older VAXes and other time-sharing systems.

THE PROPRIETARY-UNIX ERA

By 1984, when Ma Bell divested and Unix became a supported AT&T product for the first time, the most important fault line in hackerdom was between a relatively cohesive 'network nation' centered around the Internet and Usenet (and mostly using minicomputer- or workstation-class machines running Unix), and a vast disconnected hinterland of microcomputer enthusiasts.

It was also around this time that serious cracking episodes were first covered in the mainstream press—and journalists began to misapply the term "hacker" to refer to computer vandals, an abuse which sadly continues to this day.

The workstation-class machines built by Sun and others opened up new worlds for hackers. They were built to do high-performance graphics and pass around shared data over a network. During the 1980s hackerdom was preoccupied by the software and tool-building challenges of getting the most use out of these features. Berkeley Unix developed built-in support for the ARPAnet protocols, which offered a solution to the networking problems associated with UUCP's slow point-to-point links and encouraged further growth of the Internet.

There were several attempts to tame workstation graphics. The one that prevailed was the X Window System, developed at MIT with contributions from hundreds of individuals at dozens of companies. A critical factor in its success was that the X developers were willing to give the sources away for free in accordance with the hacker ethic, and able to distribute them over the Internet. X's victory over proprietary graphics systems (including one offered by Sun itself) was an important harbinger of changes that, a few years later, would profoundly affect Unix as a whole.

There was a bit of factional spleen still vented occasionally in the ITS/Unix rivalry (mostly from the ex-ITSers' side). But the last ITS machine shut down for good in 1990; the zealots no longer had a place to stand and mostly assimilated to the Unix culture with various degrees of grumbling.

Within networked hackerdom itself, the big rivalry of the 1980s was between fans of Berkeley Unix and the AT&T versions. Occasionally you can still find copies of a poster from that period, showing a cartoony X-wing fighter out of the "Star Wars" movies streaking away from an exploding Death Star patterned on the AT&T logo. Berkeley hackers liked to see themselves as rebels against soulless corporate empires. AT&T Unix never caught up with BSD/Sun in the marketplace, but it won the standards wars. By 1990, AT&T and BSD versions were becoming harder to tell apart, having adopted many of each other's innovations.

As the 1990s opened, the workstation technology of the previous decade was beginning to look distinctly threatened by newer, low-cost and high-performance personal computers based on the Intel 386 chip and its descendants. For the first time, individual hackers could afford to have home machines comparable in power and storage capacity to the minicomputers of ten years earlier—Unix engines capable of supporting a full development environment and talking to the Internet.

The MS-DOS world remained blissfully ignorant of all this. Though those early microcomputer enthusiasts quickly expanded to constitute a population of DOS and Mac hackers orders of magnitude larger than that of the network nation culture, they never became a self-aware of their culture. The pace of change was so fast that fifty different technical cultures grew and died as rapidly as mayflies, never achieving quite the stability necessary to develop a common tradition of jargon, folklore, and mythic history. The absence of a really pervasive network comparable to UUCP or Internet prevented them from becoming a network nation themselves.

Widespread access to commercial online services like CompuServe and GEnie was beginning to take hold, but the fact that non-Unix operating systems don't come bundled with development tools meant that very little source was passed over them. Thus, no tradition of collaborative hacking developed.

The mainstream of hackerdom, (dis)organized around the Internet and by now largely identified with the Unix technical culture, didn't care about the commercial services. These hackers wanted better tools and more Internet, and cheap 32-bit PCs promised to put both in everyone's reach.

But where was the software? Commercial Unixes remained expensive, in the multiple-kilobuck range. In the early 1990s several companies made a go at selling AT&T or BSD Unix ports for PC-class machines. Success was elusive, prices didn't come down much, and (worst of all) you didn't get modifiable and redistributable sources with your operating system. The traditional software-business model wasn't giving hackers what they wanted.

Neither was the Free Software Foundation. The development of HURD, RMS's long-promised free Unix kernel for hackers, got stalled for years and failed to produce anything like a usable kernel until 1996 (though by 1990 FSF supplied almost all the other difficult parts of a Unix-like operating system).

Worse, by the early 1990s it was becoming clear that ten years of effort to commercialize proprietary Unix was ending in failure. Unix's promise of cross-platform portability got lost in bickering among half a dozen proprietary Unix versions. The proprietary-Unix players proved so ponderous, so blind, and so inept at marketing that Microsoft was able to grab away a large part of their market with the shockingly inferior technology of its Windows operating system.

In early 1993, a hostile observer might have had grounds for thinking that the Unix story was almost played out, and with it the fortunes of the hacker tribe. And there was no shortage of hostile observers in the computer trade press, many of whom had been ritually predicting the imminent death of Unix at six-month intervals ever since the late 1970s.

In those days it was conventional wisdom that the era of individual techno-heroism was over, that the software industry and the nascent Internet would increasingly be dominated by colossi like Microsoft. The first generation of Unix hackers seemed to be getting old and tired (Berkeley's Computer Science Research Group ran out of steam and would lose its funding in 1994). It was a depressing time.

Fortunately, there had been things going on out of sight of the trade press, and out of sight even of most hackers, that would produce startlingly positive developments in later 1993 and 1994. Eventually, these would take the culture in a whole new direction and to undreamed-of successes.

The Early Free Unixes

Into the gap left by the Free Software Foundation's uncompleted HURD had stepped a Helsinki University student named Linus Torvalds. In 1991 he began developing a free Unix kernel for 386 machines using the Free Software Foundation's toolkit. His initial, rapid success attracted many Internet hackers to help him develop Linux, a full-featured Unix with entirely free and redistributable sources.

Linux was not without competitors. In 1991, contemporaneously with Linus Torvalds's early experiments, William and Lynne Jolitz were experimentally porting the BSD Unix sources to the 386. Most observers comparing BSD technology with Linus's crude early efforts expected that BSD ports would become the most important free Unixes on the PC.

The most important feature of Linux, however, was not technical but sociological. Until the Linux development, everyone believed that any software as complex as an operating system had to be developed in a carefully coordinated way by a relatively small, tightly-knit group of people. This model was and still is typical of both commercial software and the great freeware cathedrals built by the Free Software Foundation in the 1980s; also of the freeBSD/netBSD/OpenBSD projects that spun off from the Jolitzes' original 386BSD port.

Linux evolved in a completely different way. From nearly the beginning, it was rather casually hacked on by huge numbers of volunteers coordinating only through the Internet. Quality was maintained not by rigid standards or autocracy but by the naively simple strategy of releasing every week and getting feedback from hundreds of users within days, creating a sort of rapid Darwinian selection on the mutations introduced by developers. To the amazement of almost everyone, this worked quite well.

By late 1993 Linux could compete on stability and reliability with many commercial Unixes, and hosted vastly more software. It was even beginning to attract ports of commercial applications software. One indirect effect of this development was to kill off most of the smaller proprietary Unix vendors—without developers and hackers to sell to, they folded. One of the few survivors, BSDI (Berkeley Systems Design, Incorporated), flourished by offering full sources with its BSD-based Unix and cultivating close ties with the hacker community.

These developments were not much remarked on at the time within the hacker culture, and not at all outside it. The hacker culture, defying repeated predictions of its demise, was just beginning to remake the commercial-software world in its own image. It would be five more years, however, before this trend became obvious.

The Great Web Explosion

The early growth of Linux synergized with another phenomenon: the public discovery of the Internet. The early 1990s also saw the beginnings of a flourishing Internet-provider industry, selling connectivity to the public for a few dollars a month. Following the invention of the World Wide Web, the Internet's already rapid growth accelerated to a breakneck pace.

By 1994, the year Berkeley's Unix development group formally shut down, several different free Unix versions (Linux and the descendants of 386BSD) served as the major focal points of hacking activity. Linux was being distributed commercially on CD-ROM and selling like hotcakes. By the end of 1995, major computer companies were beginning to take out glossy advertisements celebrating the Internet-friendliness of their software and hardware!

In the late 1990s the central activities of hackerdom became Linux development and the mainstreaming of the Internet. The World Wide Web has at last made the Internet into a mass medium, and many of the hackers of the 1980s and early 1990s launched Internet Service Providers selling or giving access to the masses.

The mainstreaming of the Internet even brought the hacker culture the beginnings of respectability and political clout. In 1994 and 1995 hacker activism scuppered the Clipper proposal which would have put strong encryption under government control. In 1996 hackers mobilized a broad coalition to defeat the misnamed "Communications Decency Act" (CDA) and prevent censorship of the Internet.

With the CDA victory, we pass out of history into current events. We also pass into a period in which your historian (rather to his own surprise) became an actor rather than just an observer. This narrative will continue in *Revenge of the Hackers*.

THE CATHEDRAL AND THE BAZAAR

✦ ✦ ✦

I anatomize a successful open-source project, fetchmail, that was run as a deliberate test of the surprising theories about software engineering suggested by the history of Linux. I discuss these theories in terms of two fundamentally different development styles, the 'cathedral' model of most of the commercial world versus the 'bazaar' model of the Linux world. I show that these models derive from opposing assumptions about the nature of the software-debugging task. I then make a sustained argument from the Linux experience for the proposition that "Given enough eyeballs, all bugs are shallow", suggest productive analogies with other self-correcting systems of selfish agents, and conclude with some exploration of the implications of this insight for the future of software.

THE CATHEDRAL AND THE BAZAAR

Linux is subversive. Who would have thought even five years ago (1991) that a world-class operating system could coalesce as if by magic out of part-time hacking by several thousand developers scattered all over the planet, connected only by the tenuous strands of the Internet?

Certainly not I. By the time Linux swam onto my radar screen in early 1993, I had already been involved in Unix and open-source development for 10 years. I was one of the first GNU contributors in the mid-1980s. I had released a good deal of open-source software onto the Net, developing or co-developing several programs (nethack, Emacs's VC and GUD modes, xlife, and others) that are still in wide use today. I thought I knew how it was done.

Linux overturned much of what I thought I knew. I had been preaching the Unix gospel of small tools, rapid prototyping, and evolutionary programming for years. But I also believed there was a certain critical complexity above which a more centralized, *a priori* approach was required. I believed that the most important software (operating systems and really large tools like the Emacs programming editor) needed to be built like cathedrals, carefully crafted by individual wizards or small bands of mages working in splendid isolation, with no beta to be released before its time.

Linus Torvalds's style of development—release early and often, delegate everything you can, be open to the point of promiscuity—came as a surprise. No quiet, reverent cathedral-building here—rather, the Linux community seemed to resemble a great babbling bazaar of differing agendas and approaches (aptly symbolized by the Linux archive sites, which would take submissions from *anyone*) out of which a coherent and stable system could seemingly emerge only by a succession of miracles.

The fact that this bazaar style seemed to work, and work well, came as a distinct shock. As I learned my way around, I worked hard not just at individual projects, but also at trying to understand why the Linux world not only didn't fly apart in confusion but seemed to go from strength to strength at a speed barely imaginable to cathedral-builders.

By mid-1996 I thought I was beginning to understand. Chance handed me a perfect way to test my theory, in the form of an open-source project that I could consciously try to run in the bazaar style. So I did—and it was a significant success.

This is the story of that project. I'll use it to propose some aphorisms about effective open-source development. Not all of these are things I first learned in the Linux world, but we'll see how the Linux world gives them particular point. If I'm correct, they'll help you understand exactly what it is that makes the Linux community such a fountain of good software—and, perhaps, they will help you become more productive yourself.

THE MAIL MUST GET THROUGH

Since 1993 I'd been running the technical side of a small free-access Internet service provider called Chester County InterLink (CCIL) in West Chester, Pennsylvania. I co-founded CCIL and wrote our unique multiuser bulletin-board software—you can check it out by telnetting to *locke.ccil.org*. Today it supports almost 3000 users on 30 lines. The job allowed me 24-hour-a-day access to the net through CCIL's 56K line—in fact, the job practically demanded it!

I had gotten quite used to instant Internet email. I found having to periodically telnet over to locke to check my mail annoying. What I wanted was for my mail to be delivered on snark (my home system) so that I would be notified when it arrived and could handle it using all my local tools.

The Internet's native mail forwarding protocol, SMTP (Simple Mail Transfer Protocol), wouldn't suit, because it works best when machines are connected full-time, while my personal machine isn't always on the Internet and doesn't have a static IP address. What I needed was a program that would reach out over my intermittent dialup connection and pull across my mail to be delivered locally. I knew such things existed, and that most of them used a simple application protocol called POP (Post Office Protocol). POP is now widely supported by most common mail clients, but at the time, it wasn't built in to the mail reader I was using.

I needed a POP3 client. So I went out on the Internet and found one. Actually, I found three or four. I used one of them for a while, but it was missing what seemed an obvious feature, the ability to hack the addresses on fetched mail so replies would work properly.

The problem was this: suppose someone named joe on locke sent me mail. If I fetched the mail to snark and then tried to reply to it, my mailer would cheerfully try to ship it to a nonexistent joe on snark. Hand-editing reply addresses to tack on *@ccil.org* quickly got to be a serious pain.

This was clearly something the computer ought to be doing for me. But none of the existing POP clients knew how! And this brings us to the first lesson:

1. EVERY GOOD WORK OF SOFTWARE STARTS BY SCRATCH-ING A DEVELOPER'S PERSONAL ITCH.

Perhaps this should have been obvious (it's long been proverbial that "Necessity is the mother of invention"), but too often software developers spend their days grinding away for pay at programs they neither need nor love. But not in the Linux world—which may explain why the average quality of software originated in the Linux community is so high.

So, did I immediately launch into a furious whirl of coding up a brand-new POP3 client to compete with the existing ones? Not on your life! I looked carefully at the POP utilities I had in hand, asking myself "Which one is closest to what I want?" Because:

2. GOOD PROGRAMMERS KNOW WHAT TO WRITE. GREAT ONES KNOW WHAT TO REWRITE (AND REUSE).

While I don't claim to be a great programmer, I try to imitate one. An important trait of the great ones is constructive laziness. They know that you get an A not for effort but for results, and that it's almost always easier to start from a good partial solution than from nothing at all.

Linus Torvalds (*http://www.tuxedo.org/~esr/faqs/linus*), for example, didn't actually try to write Linux from scratch. Instead, he started by reusing code and ideas from Minix, a tiny Unix-like operating system for PC clones. Eventually all the Minix code went away or was completely rewritten—but while it was there, it provided scaffolding for the infant that would eventually become Linux.

In the same spirit, I went looking for an existing POP utility that was reasonably well coded, to use as a development base.

The source-sharing tradition of the Unix world has always been friendly to code reuse (this is why the GNU project chose Unix as a base OS, in spite of serious reservations about the OS itself). The Linux world has taken this tradition nearly to its technological limit; it has terabytes of open sources generally available. So spending time looking for someone else's almost-good-enough is more likely to give you good results in the Linux world than anywhere else.

And it did for me. With those I'd found earlier, my second search made up a total of nine candidates—fetchpop, PopTart, get-mail, gwpop, pimp, pop-perl, popc, popmail and upop. The one I first settled on was 'fetchpop' by Seung-Hong Oh. I put my header-rewrite feature in it, and made various other improvements that the author accepted into his 1.9 release.

Just a few weeks later, though, I stumbled across the code for popclient by Carl Harris, and found I had a problem. Though fetchpop had some good original ideas in it (such as its background-daemon mode), it could only handle POP3 and was rather amateurishly coded (Seung-Hong was at that time a bright but inexperienced programmer, and both traits showed). Carl's code was better, quite professional and solid, but his program lacked several important and rather tricky-to-implement fetchpop features (including those I'd coded myself).

Stay or switch? If I switched, I'd be throwing away the coding I'd already done in exchange for a better development base.

A practical motive to switch was the presence of multiple-protocol support. POP3 is the most commonly used of the post-office server protocols, but not the only one. Fetchpop and the other competition didn't do POP2, RPOP, or APOP, and I was already having vague thoughts of perhaps adding IMAP (Internet Message Access Protocol, the most recently designed and most powerful post-office protocol, *http://www.imap.org*) just for fun.

But I had a more theoretical reason to think switching might be as good an idea as well, something I learned long before Linux.

3. "PLAN TO THROW ONE AWAY; YOU WILL, ANYHOW."
(FRED BROOKS, *The Mythical Man-Month*, Chapter 11)

Or, to put it another way, you often don't really understand the problem until after the first time you implement a solution. The second time, maybe you know enough to do it right. So if you want to get it right, be ready to start over *at least* once [1].

Well (I told myself) the changes to fetchpop had been my first try. So I switched.

After I sent my first set of popclient patches to Carl Harris on 25 June 1996, I found out that he had basically lost interest in popclient some time before. The code was a bit dusty, with minor bugs hanging out. I had many changes to make, and we quickly agreed that the logical thing for me to do was take over the program.

Without my actually noticing, the project had escalated. No longer was I just contemplating minor patches to an existing POP client. I took on maintaining an entire one, and there were ideas bubbling in my head that I knew would probably lead to major changes.

In a software culture that encourages code-sharing, this is a natural way for a project to evolve. I was acting out this principle:

> 4. If you have the right attitude, interesting problems will find you.

But Carl Harris's attitude was even more important. He understood that:

> 5. When you lose interest in a program, your last duty to it is to hand it off to a competent successor.

Without ever having to discuss it, Carl and I knew we had a common goal of having the best solution out there. The only question for either of us was whether I could establish that I was a safe pair of hands. Once I did that, he acted with grace and dispatch. I hope I will do as well when it comes my turn.

The Importance of Having Users

And so I inherited popclient. Just as importantly, I inherited popclient's user base. Users are wonderful things to have, and not just because they demonstrate that you're serving a need, that you've done something right. Properly cultivated, they can become co-developers.

Another strength of the Unix tradition, one that Linux pushes to a happy extreme, is that a lot of users are hackers too. Because source code is available, they can be *effective* hackers. This can be tremendously useful for shortening debugging time. Given a bit of encouragement, your users will diagnose problems, suggest fixes, and help improve the code far more quickly than you could unaided.

6. TREATING YOUR USERS AS CO-DEVELOPERS IS YOUR LEAST-HASSLE ROUTE TO RAPID CODE IMPROVEMENT AND EFFECTIVE DEBUGGING.

The power of this effect is easy to underestimate. In fact, pretty well all of us in the open-source world drastically underestimated how well it would scale up with number of users and against system complexity, until Linus Torvalds showed us differently.

In fact, I think Linus's cleverest and most consequential hack was not the construction of the Linux kernel itself, but rather his invention of the Linux development model. When I expressed this opinion in his presence once, he smiled and quietly repeated something he has often said: "I'm basically a very lazy person who likes to get credit for things other people actually do." Lazy like a fox. Or, as Robert Heinlein famously wrote of one of his characters, too lazy to fail.

In retrospect, one precedent for the methods and success of Linux can be seen in the development of the GNU Emacs Lisp library and Lisp code archives. In contrast to the cathedral-building style of the Emacs C core and most other GNU tools, the evolution of the Lisp code pool was fluid and very user-driven. Ideas and prototype modes were often rewritten three or four times before reaching a stable final form. And loosely-coupled collaborations enabled by the Internet, *a la* Linux, were frequent.

Indeed, my own most successful single hack previous to fetchmail was probably Emacs VC (version control) mode, a Linux-like collaboration by email with three other people, only one of whom (Richard Stallman, the author of Emacs and founder of the Free

Software Foundation, (*http://www.fsf.org*") I have met to this day. It was a front-end for SCCS, RCS, and later CVS from within Emacs that offered "one-touch" version control operations. It evolved from a tiny, crude sccs.el mode somebody else had written. And the development of VC succeeded because, unlike Emacs itself, Emacs Lisp code could go through release/test/improve generations very quickly.

The Emacs story is not unique. There have been other software products with a two-level architecture and a two-tier user community that combined a cathedral-mode core and a bazaar-mode toolbox. One such is MATLAB, a commercial data-analysis and visualization tool. Users of MATLAB and other products with a similar structure invariably report that the action, the ferment, the innovation mostly takes place in the open part of the tool where a large and varied community can tinker with it.

RELEASE EARLY, RELEASE OFTEN

Early and frequent releases are a critical part of the Linux development model. Most developers (including me) used to believe this was bad policy for larger than trivial projects, because early versions are almost by definition buggy versions and you don't want to wear out the patience of your users.

This belief reinforced the general commitment to a cathedral-building style of development. If the overriding objective was for users to see as few bugs as possible, why then you'd only release a version every six months (or less often), and work like a dog on debugging between releases. The Emacs C core was developed this way. The Lisp library, in effect, was not—because there were active Lisp archives outside the FSF's control, where you could go to find new and development code versions independently of Emacs's release cycle [2].

The most important of these, the Ohio State Emacs Lisp archive, anticipated the spirit and many of the features of today's big Linux archives. But few of us really thought very hard about what we were doing, or about what the very existence of that archive suggested about problems in the FSF's cathedral-building development model. I made one serious attempt around 1992 to get a lot of the Ohio code formally merged into the official Emacs Lisp library. I ran into political trouble and was largely unsuccessful.

But by a year later, as Linux became widely visible, it was clear that something different and much healthier was going on there. Linus's open development policy was the very opposite of cathedral-building. Linux's Internet archives were burgeoning, multiple distributions were being floated. And all of this was driven by an unheard-of frequency of core system releases.

Linus was treating his users as co-developers in the most effective possible way:

> 7. RELEASE EARLY. RELEASE OFTEN. AND LISTEN TO YOUR CUSTOMERS.

Linus's innovation wasn't so much in doing quick-turnaround releases incorporating lots of user feedback (something like this had been Unix-world tradition for a long time), but in scaling it up to a level of intensity that matched the complexity of what he was developing. In those early times (around 1991) it wasn't unknown for him to release a new kernel more than once a *day!* Because he cultivated his base of co-developers and leveraged the Internet for collaboration harder than anyone else, this worked.

But *how* did it work? And was it something I could duplicate, or did it rely on some unique genius of Linus Torvalds?

I didn't think so. Granted, Linus is a damn fine hacker. How many of us could engineer an entire production-quality operating system kernel from scratch? But Linux didn't represent any awesome conceptual leap forward. Linus is not (or at least, not yet) an innovative genius of design in the way that, say, Richard Stallman or James Gosling (of NeWS and Java) are. Rather, Linus seems to me to be a genius of engineering and implementation, with a sixth sense for avoiding bugs and development dead-ends and a true knack for finding the minimum-effort path from point A to point B. Indeed, the whole design of Linux breathes this quality and mirrors Linus's essentially conservative and simplifying design approach.

So, if rapid releases and leveraging the Internet medium to the hilt were not accidents but integral parts of Linus's engineering-genius insight into the minimum-effort path, what was he maximizing? What was he cranking out of the machinery?

Put that way, the question answers itself. Linus was keeping his hacker/users constantly stimulated and rewarded—stimulated by the prospect of having an ego-satisfying piece of the action, rewarded by the sight of constant (even *daily*) improvement in their work.

Linus was directly aiming to maximize the number of person-hours thrown at debugging and development, even at the possible cost of instability in the code and user-base burnout if any serious bug proved intractable. Linus was behaving as though he believed something like this:

8. GIVEN A LARGE ENOUGH BETA-TESTER AND CO-DEVELOPER BASE, ALMOST EVERY PROBLEM WILL BE CHARACTERIZED QUICKLY AND THE FIX OBVIOUS TO SOMEONE.

Or, less formally, "Given enough eyeballs, all bugs are shallow." I dub this: "Linus's Law".

My original formulation was that every problem "will be transparent to somebody". Linus demurred that the person who understands and fixes the problem is not necessarily or even usually the person who first characterizes it. "Somebody finds the problem," he says, "and somebody *else* understands it. And I'll go on record as saying that finding it is the bigger challenge." That correction is important; we'll see how in the next section, when we examine the practice of debugging in more detail. But the key point is that both parts of the process (finding and fixing) tend to happen rapidly.

In Linus's Law, I think, lies the core difference underlying the cathedral-builder and bazaar styles. In the cathedral-builder view of programming, bugs and development problems are tricky, insidious, deep phenomena. It takes months of scrutiny by a dedicated few to develop confidence that you've winkled them all out. Thus the long release intervals, and the inevitable disappointment when long-awaited releases are not perfect.

In the bazaar view, on the other hand, you assume that bugs are generally shallow phenomena—or, at least, that they turn shallow pretty quickly when exposed to a thousand eager co-developers pounding on every single new release. Accordingly you release often in order to get more corrections, and as a beneficial side effect you have less to lose if an occasional botch gets out the door.

And that's it. That's enough. If "Linus's Law" is false, then any system as complex as the Linux kernel, being hacked over by as many hands as that kernel was, should at some point have collapsed under the weight of unforseen bad interactions and undiscovered "deep" bugs. If it's true, on the other hand, it is sufficient to explain Linux's relative lack of bugginess and its continuous uptimes spanning months or even years.

Maybe it shouldn't have been such a surprise, at that. Sociologists years ago discovered that the averaged opinion of a mass of equally expert (or equally ignorant) observers is quite a bit more reliable a predictor than the opinion of a single randomly chosen observer. They called this the *Delphi effect*. It appears that what Linus has shown is that this applies even to debugging an operating system—that the Delphi effect can tame development complexity even at the complexity level of an OS kernel [3].

One special feature of the Linux situation that clearly helps along the Delphi effect is the fact that the contributors for any given project are self-selected. An early respondent pointed out that contributions are received not from a random sample, but from people who are interested enough to use the software, learn about how it works, attempt to find solutions to problems they encounter, and actually produce an apparently reasonable fix. Anyone who passes all these filters is highly likely to have something useful to contribute.

Linus's Law can be rephrased as "Debugging is parallelizable". Although debugging requires debuggers to communicate with some coordinating developer, it doesn't require significant coordination between debuggers. Thus it doesn't fall prey to the same quadratic complexity and management costs that make adding developers problematic.

In practice, the theoretical loss of efficiency due to duplication of work by debuggers almost never seems to be an issue in the Linux world. One effect of a "release early and often" policy is to minimize such duplication by propagating fed-back fixes quickly [4].

Brooks (the author of *The Mythical Man-Month*) even made an off-hand observation related to Jeff's: "The total cost of maintaining a widely used program is typically 40 percent or more of the cost of developing it. Surprisingly this cost is strongly affected by the number of users. *More users find more bugs.*" [Emphasis added.]

More users find more bugs because adding more users adds more different ways of stressing the program. This effect is amplified when the users are co-developers. Each one approaches the task of bug characterization with a slightly different perceptual set and analytical toolkit, a different angle on the problem. The Delphi Effect seems to work precisely because of this variation. In the specific context of debugging, the variation also tends to reduce duplication of effort.

So adding more beta-testers may not reduce the complexity of the current "deepest" bug from the *developer's* point of view, but it increases the probability that someone's toolkit will be matched to the problem in such a way that the bug is shallow *to that person*.

Linus coppers his bets, too. In case there *are* serious bugs, Linux kernel version are numbered in such a way that potential users can make a choice either to run the last version designated "stable" or to ride the cutting edge and risk bugs in order to get new features. This tactic is not yet systematically imitated by most Linux hackers, but perhaps it should be; the fact that either choice is available makes both more attractive [5].

MANY EYEBALLS TAME COMPLEXITY

It's one thing to observe in the large that the bazaar style greatly accelerates debugging and code evolution. It's another to understand exactly how and why it does so at the micro-level of day-to-day developer and tester behavior. In this section (written three years after the original paper, using insights by developers who read it and re-examined their own behavior) we'll take a hard look at the actual mechanisms. Non-technically inclined readers can safely skip to the next section.

One key to understanding is to realize exactly why it is that the kind of bug report non–source-aware users normally turn in tends not to be very useful. Non–source-aware users tend to report only surface symptoms; they take their environment for granted, so they (a) omit critical background data, and (b) seldom include a reliable recipe for reproducing the bug.

The underlying problem here is a mismatch between the tester's and the developer's mental models of the program; the tester, on the outside looking in, and the developer on the inside looking out. In closed-source development they're both stuck in these roles, and tend to talk past each other and find each other deeply frustrating.

Open-source development breaks this bind, making it far easier for tester and developer to develop a shared representation grounded in the actual source code and to communicate effectively about it. Practically, there is a huge difference in leverage for the developer between the kind of bug report that just reports externally visible symptoms and the kind that hooks directly to the developer's source-code–based mental representation of the program.

Most bugs, most of the time, are easily nailed given even an incomplete but suggestive characterization of their error conditions at source-code level. When someone among your beta-testers can point out, "there's a boundary problem in line nnn", or even just "under conditions X, Y, and Z, this variable rolls over", a quick look at the offending code often suffices to pin down the exact mode of failure and generate a fix.

Thus, source-code awareness by both parties greatly enhances both good communication and the synergy between what a beta-tester reports and what the core developer(s) knows. In turn, this means that the core developers' time tends to be well conserved, even with many collaborators.

Another characteristic of the open-source method that conserves developer time is the communication structure of typical open-source projects. Earlier I used the term "core developer"; this reflects a distinction between the project core (typically quite small; a single core developer is common, and one to three is typical) and the project halo of beta-testers and available contributors (which often numbers in the hundreds).

The fundamental problem that traditional software-development organization addresses is Brooks's Law: "Adding more programmers to a late project makes it later." More generally, Brooks's Law predicts that the complexity and communication costs of a project rise with the square of the number of developers, while work done only rises linearly.

Brooks's Law is founded on experience that bugs tend strongly to cluster at the interfaces between code written by different people, and that communications/coordination overhead on a project tends to rise with the number of interfaces between human beings. Thus, problems scale with the number of communications paths between developers, which scales as the square of the number of developers (more precisely, according to the formula $N*(N-1)/2$ where N is the number of developers).

The Brooks's Law analysis (and the resulting fear of large numbers in development groups) rests on a hidden assummption: that the communications structure of the project is necessarily a complete graph, that everybody talks to everybody else. But on open-source projects, the halo developers work on what are in effect separable parallel subtasks and interact with each other very little; code changes and bug reports stream through the core group, and only *within* that small core group do we pay the full Brooksian overhead [6].

There are are still more reasons that source-code–level bug reporting tends to be very efficient. They center around the fact that a single error can often have multiple possible symptoms, manifesting differently depending on details of the user's usage pattern and environment. Such errors tend to be exactly the sort of complex and subtle bugs (such as dynamic-memory-management errors or nondeterministic interrupt-window artifacts) that are hardest to reproduce at will or to pin down by static analysis, and which do the most to create long-term problems in software.

A tester who sends in a tentative source-code–level characterization of such a multi-symptom bug (e.g., "It looks to me like there's a window in the signal handling near line 1250" or "Where are you zeroing that buffer?") may give a developer, otherwise too close to the code to see it, the critical clue to a half-dozen disparate symptoms. In cases like this, it may be hard or even impossible to know which externally visible misbehaviour was caused by precisely which bug—but with frequent releases, it's unnecessary to know. Other collaborators will be likely to find out quickly whether their bug has been fixed or not. In many cases, source-level bug reports will cause misbehaviours to drop out without ever having been attributed to any specific fix.

Complex multi-symptom errors also tend to have multiple trace paths from surface symptoms back to the actual bug. Which of the trace paths a given developer or tester can chase may depend on subtleties of that person's environment, and may well change in a not obviously deterministic way over time. In effect, each developer and tester samples a semi-random set of the program's state space when looking for the etiology of a symptom. The more subtle and complex the bug, the less likely that skill will be able to guarantee the relevance of that sample.

For simple and easily reproducible bugs, then, the accent will be on the "semi" rather than the "random"; debugging skill and intimacy with the code and its architecture will matter a lot. But for complex bugs, the accent will be on the "random". Under these circumstances many people running traces will be much more effective than a few people running traces sequentially—even if the few have a much higher average skill level.

This effect will be greatly amplified if the difficulty of following trace paths from different surface symptoms back to a bug varies significantly in a way that can't be predicted by looking at the symptoms. A single developer sampling those paths sequentially will be as likely to pick a difficult trace path on the first try as an easy one. On the other hand, suppose many people are trying trace paths in parallel while doing rapid releases. Then it is likely one of them will find the easiest path immediately, and nail the bug in a much shorter time. The project maintainer will see that, ship a new release, and the other people running traces on the same bug will be able to stop before having spent too much time on their more difficult traces [7].

WHEN IS A ROSE NOT A ROSE?

Having studied Linus's behavior and formed a theory about why it was successful, I made a conscious decision to test this theory on my new (admittedly much less complex and ambitious) project.

But the first thing I did was reorganize and simplify popclient a lot. Carl Harris's implementation was very sound, but exhibited a kind of unnecessary complexity common to many C programmers. He treated the code as central and the data structures as support for the code. As a result, the code was beautiful but the data structure design *ad hoc* and rather ugly (at least by the high standards of this veteran LISP hacker).

I had another purpose for rewriting besides improving the code and the data structure design, however. That was to evolve it into something I understood completely. It's no fun to be responsible for fixing bugs in a program you don't understand.

For the first month or so, then, I was simply following out the implications of Carl's basic design. The first serious change I made was to add IMAP support. I did this by reorganizing the protocol machines into a generic driver and three method tables (for POP2, POP3, and IMAP). This and the previous changes illustrate a general principle that's good for programmers to keep in mind, especially in languages like C that don't naturally do dynamic typing:

9. SMART DATA STRUCTURES AND DUMB CODE WORKS A LOT BETTER THAN THE OTHER WAY AROUND.

Brooks, Chapter 9: "Show me your flowchart and conceal your tables, and I shall continue to be mystified. Show me your tables, and I won't usually need your flowchart; it'll be obvious." Allowing for 30 years of terminological/cultural shift, it's the same point.

At this point (early September 1996, about six weeks from zero) I started thinking that a name change might be in order—after all, it wasn't just a POP client any more. But I hesitated, because there was as yet nothing genuinely new in the design. My version of popclient had yet to develop an identity of its own.

That changed, radically, when popclient learned how to forward fetched mail to the SMTP port. I'll get to that in a moment. But first: I said earlier that I'd decided to use this project to test my theory about what Linus Torvalds had done right. How (you may well ask) did I do that? In these ways:

- I released early and often (almost never less often than every 10 days; during periods of intense development, once a day).
- I grew my beta list by adding to it everyone who contacted me about fetchmail.
- I sent chatty announcements to the beta list whenever I released, encouraging people to participate.
- I listened to my beta-testers, polling them about design decisions and stroking them whenever they sent in patches and feedback.

The payoff from these simple measures was immediate. From the beginning of the project, I got bug reports of a quality most developers would kill for, often with good fixes attached. I got thoughtful criticism, I got fan mail, I got intelligent feature suggestions. Which leads to:

10.If you treat your beta-testers as if they're your most valuable resource, they will respond by becoming your most valuable resource.

One interesting measure of fetchmail's success is the sheer size of the project beta list, fetchmail-friends. At the time of latest revision of this paper (November 2000) it has 287 members and is adding 2 or 3 a week.

Actually, when I revised in late May 1997 I found the list was beginning to lose members from its high of close to 300 for an interesting reason. Several people have asked me to unsubscribe them because fetchmail is working so well for them that they no longer need to see the list traffic! Perhaps this is part of the normal life-cycle of a mature bazaar-style project.

POPCLIENT BECOMES FETCHMAIL

The real turning point in the project was when Harry Hochheiser sent me his scratch code for forwarding mail to the client machine's SMTP port. I realized almost immediately that a reliable implementation of this feature would make all the other mail delivery modes next to obsolete.

For many weeks I had been tweaking fetchmail rather incrementally while feeling like the interface design was serviceable but grubby—inelegant and with too many exiguous options hanging out all over. The options to dump fetched mail to a mailbox file or standard output particularly bothered me, but I couldn't figure out why.

(If you don't care about the technicalia of Internet mail, the next two paragraphs can be safely skipped.)

What I saw when I thought about SMTP forwarding was that popclient had been trying to do too many things. It had been designed to be both a mail transport agent (MTA) and a local delivery agent (MDA). With SMTP forwarding, it could get out of the MDA business and be a pure MTA, handing off mail to other programs for local delivery just as sendmail does.

Why mess with all the complexity of configuring a mail delivery agent or setting up lock-and-append on a mailbox when port 25 is almost guaranteed to be there on any platform with TCP/IP support in the first place? Especially when this means retrieved mail is guaranteed to look like normal sender-initiated SMTP mail, which is really what we want anyway.

(Back to a higher level . . .)

Even if you didn't follow the preceding technical jargon, there are several important lessons here. First, this SMTP-forwarding concept was the biggest single payoff I got from consciously trying to emulate Linus's methods. A user gave me this terrific idea—all I had to do was understand the implications.

11.THE NEXT BEST THING TO HAVING GOOD IDEAS IS REC-
OGNIZING GOOD IDEAS FROM YOUR USERS. SOMETIMES
THE LATTER IS BETTER.

Interestingly enough, you will quickly find that if you are completely and self-deprecatingly truthful about how much you owe
other people, the world at large will treat you as though you did
every bit of the invention yourself and are just being becomingly
modest about your innate genius. We can all see how well this
worked for Linus!

(When I gave my talk at the first Perl Conference in August 1997,
hacker extraordinaire Larry Wall was in the front row. As I got to
the last line above he called out, religious-revival style, "Tell it, tell
it, brother!" The whole audience laughed, because they knew this
had worked for the inventor of Perl, too.)

After a few weeks of running the project in the same spirit, I
began to get similar praise not just from my users but from other
people to whom the word leaked out. I stashed away some of that
email; I'll look at it again sometime if I ever start wondering
whether my life has been worthwhile :-).

But there are two more fundamental, non-political lessons here
that are general to all kinds of design.

12.OFTEN, THE MOST STRIKING AND INNOVATIVE SOLU-
TIONS COME FROM REALIZING THAT YOUR CONCEPT OF
THE PROBLEM WAS WRONG.

I had been trying to solve the wrong problem by continuing to
develop popclient as a combined MTA/MDA with all kinds of
funky local delivery modes. Fetchmail's design needed to be
rethought from the ground up as a pure MTA, a part of the normal SMTP-speaking Internet mail path.

When you hit a wall in development—when you find yourself
hard put to think past the next patch—it's often time to ask not
whether you've got the right answer, but whether you're asking
the right question. Perhaps the problem needs to be reframed.

Well, I had reframed my problem. Clearly, the right thing to do was (1) hack SMTP forwarding support into the generic driver, (2) make it the default mode, and (3) eventually throw out all the other delivery modes, especially the deliver-to-file and deliver-to-standard-output options.

I hesitated over step 3 for some time, fearing to upset long-time popclient users dependent on the alternate delivery mechanisms. In theory, they could immediately switch to *.forward* files or their non-sendmail equivalents to get the same effects. In practice the transition might have been messy.

But when I did it, the benefits proved huge. The cruftiest parts of the driver code vanished. Configuration got radically simpler—no more grovelling around for the system MDA and user's mailbox, no more worries about whether the underlying OS supports file locking.

Also, the only way to lose mail vanished. If you specified delivery to a file and the disk got full, your mail got lost. This can't happen with SMTP forwarding because your SMTP listener won't return OK unless the message can be delivered or at least spooled for later delivery.

Also, performance improved (though not so you'd notice it in a single run). Another not insignificant benefit of this change was that the manual page got a lot simpler.

Later, I had to bring delivery via a user-specified local MDA back in order to allow handling of some obscure situations involving dynamic SLIP. But I found a much simpler way to do it.

The moral? Don't hesitate to throw away superannuated features when you can do it without loss of effectiveness. Antoine de Saint-Exupéry (who was an aviator and aircraft designer when he wasn't authoring classic children's books) said:

> 13. "PERFECTION (IN DESIGN) IS ACHIEVED NOT WHEN THERE IS NOTHING MORE TO ADD, BUT RATHER WHEN THERE IS NOTHING MORE TO TAKE AWAY."

When your code is getting both better and simpler, that is when you *know* it's right. And in the process, the fetchmail design acquired an identity of its own, different from the ancestral popclient.

It was time for the name change. The new design looked much more like a dual of sendmail than the old popclient had; both are MTAs, but where sendmail pushes then delivers, the new popclient pulls then delivers. So, two months off the blocks, I renamed it fetchmail.

There is a more general lesson in this story about how SMTP delivery came to fetchmail. It is not only debugging that is parallelizable; development and (to a perhaps surprising extent) exploration of design space is, too. When your development mode is rapidly iterative, development and enhancement may become special cases of debugging—fixing 'bugs of omission' in the original capabilities or concept of the software.

Even at a higher level of design, it can be very valuable to have lots of co-developers random-walking through the design space near your product. Consider the way a puddle of water finds a drain, or better yet how ants find food: exploration essentially by diffusion, followed by exploitation mediated by a scalable communication mechanism. This works very well; as with Harry Hochheiser and me, one of your outriders may well find a huge win nearby that you were just a little too close-focused to see.

FETCHMAIL GROWS UP

There I was with a neat and innovative design, code that I knew worked well because I used it every day, and a burgeoning beta list. It gradually dawned on me that I was no longer engaged in a trivial personal hack that might happen to be useful to few other people. I had my hands on a program that every hacker with a Unix box and a SLIP/PPP mail connection really needs.

With the SMTP forwarding feature, it pulled far enough in front of the competition to potentially become a category killer, one of those classic programs that fills its niche so competently that the alternatives are not just discarded but almost forgotten.

I think you can't really aim or plan for a result like this. You have to get pulled into it by design ideas so powerful that afterward the results just seem inevitable, natural, even foreordained. The only way to try for ideas like that is by having lots of ideas—or by having the engineering judgment to take other people's good ideas beyond where the originators thought they could go.

Andy Tanenbaum had the original idea to build a simple native Unix for IBM PCs, for use as a teaching tool (he called it Minix). Linus Torvalds pushed the Minix concept further than Andrew probably thought it could go—and it grew into something wonderful. In the same way (though on a smaller scale), I took some ideas by Carl Harris and Harry Hochheiser and pushed them hard. Neither of us was original in the romantic way people think is genius. But then, most science and engineering and software development isn't done by original genius, hacker mythology to the contrary.

The results were pretty heady stuff all the same—in fact, just the kind of success every hacker lives for! And they meant I would have to set my standards even higher. To make fetchmail as good as I now saw it could be, I'd have to write not just for my own needs, but also include and support features necessary to others outside my orbit. And do that while keeping the program simple and robust.

The first and overwhelmingly most important feature I wrote after realizing this was multidrop support—the ability to fetch mail from mailboxes that had accumulated all mail for a group of users, and then route each piece of mail to its individual recipients.

I decided to add the multidrop support partly because some users were clamoring for it, but mostly because I thought it would shake bugs out of the single-drop code by forcing me to deal with addressing in full generality. And so it proved. Getting RFC 822 (*http://info.internet.isi.edu:80/in-notes/rfc/files/rfc822.txt*) address parsing right took me a remarkably long time, not because any individual piece of it is hard but because it involved a pile of inter-dependent and fussy details.

But multidrop addressing turned out to be an excellent design decision as well. Here's how I knew:

14.ANY TOOL SHOULD BE USEFUL IN THE EXPECTED WAY, BUT A TRULY GREAT TOOL LENDS ITSELF TO USES YOU NEVER EXPECTED.

The unexpected use for multidrop fetchmail is to run mailing lists with the list kept, and alias expansion done, on the *client* side of the Internet connection. This means someone running a personal machine through an ISP account can manage a mailing list without continuing access to the ISP's alias files.

Another important change demanded by my beta-testers was support for 8-bit MIME (Multipurpose Internet Mail Extensions) operation. This was pretty easy to do, because I had been careful to keep the code 8-bit clean (that is, to not press the 8th bit, unused in the ASCII character set, into service to carry information within the program). Not because I anticipated the demand for this feature, but rather in obedience to another rule:

15.WHEN WRITING GATEWAY SOFTWARE OF ANY KIND, TAKE PAINS TO DISTURB THE DATA STREAM AS LITTLE AS POS-SIBLE — AND *never* throw away information unless the recipient forces you to!

Had I not obeyed this rule, 8-bit MIME support would have been difficult and buggy. As it was, all I had to do is read the MIME standard (RFC 1652, *http://info.internet.isi.edu:80/in-notes/rfc/files/rfc1652.txt*) and add a trivial bit of header-generation logic.

Some European users bugged me into adding an option to limit the number of messages retrieved per session (so they can control costs from their expensive phone networks). I resisted this for a long time, and I'm still not entirely happy about it. But if you're writing for the world, you have to listen to your customers—this doesn't change just because they're not paying you in money.

A FEW MORE LESSONS FROM FETCHMAIL

Before we go back to general software-engineering issues, there are a couple more specific lessons from the fetchmail experience to ponder. Nontechnical readers can safely skip this section.

The rc (control) file syntax includes optional 'noise' keywords that are entirely ignored by the parser. The English-like syntax they allow is considerably more readable than the traditional terse keyword-value pairs you get when you strip them all out.

These started out as a late-night experiment when I noticed how much the rc file declarations were beginning to resemble an imperative minilanguage. (This is also why I changed the original popclient "server" keyword to "poll").

It seemed to me that trying to make that imperative minilanguage more like English might make it easier to use. Now, although I'm a convinced partisan of the "make it a language" school of design as exemplified by Emacs and HTML and many database engines, I am not normally a big fan of "English-like" syntaxes.

Traditionally programmers have tended to favor control syntaxes that are very precise and compact and have no redundancy at all. This is a cultural legacy from when computing resources were expensive, so parsing stages had to be as cheap and simple as possible. English, with about 50% redundancy, looked like a very inappropriate model then.

This is not my reason for normally avoiding English-like syntaxes; I mention it here only to demolish it. With cheap cycles and core, terseness should not be an end in itself. Nowadays it's more important for a language to be convenient for humans than to be cheap for the computer.

There remain, however, good reasons to be wary. One is the complexity cost of the parsing stage—you don't want to raise that to the point where it's a significant source of bugs and user confusion in itself. Another is that trying to make a language syntax English-like often demands that the "English" it speaks be bent seriously out of shape, so much so that the superficial resemblance to natural language is as confusing as a traditional syntax would have been. (You see this bad effect in a lot of so-called "fourth generation" and commercial database-query languages.)

The fetchmail control syntax seems to avoid these problems because the language domain is extremely restricted. It's nowhere near a general-purpose language; the things it says simply are not very complicated, so there's little potential for confusion in moving mentally between a tiny subset of English and the actual control language. I think there may be a broader lesson here:

16. WHEN YOUR LANGUAGE IS NOWHERE NEAR TURING-COMPLETE, SYNTACTIC SUGAR CAN BE YOUR FRIEND.

Another lesson is about security by obscurity. Some fetchmail users asked me to change the software to store passwords encrypted in the rc file, so snoopers wouldn't be able to casually see them.

I didn't do it, because this doesn't actually add protection. Anyone who's acquired permissions to read your rc file will be able to run fetchmail as you anyway—and if it's your password they're after, they'd be able to rip the necessary decoder out of the fetchmail code itself to get it.

All *.fetchmailrc* password encryption would have done is give a false sense of security to people who don't think very hard. The general rule here is:

17. A SECURITY SYSTEM IS ONLY AS SECURE AS ITS SECRET. BEWARE OF PSEUDO-SECRETS.

NECESSARY PRECONDITIONS
FOR THE BAZAAR STYLE

Early reviewers and test audiences for this essay consistently raised questions about the preconditions for successful bazaar-style development, including both the qualifications of the project leader and the state of code at the time one goes public and starts to try to build a co-developer community.

It's fairly clear that one cannot code from the ground up in bazaar style [8]. One can test, debug and improve in bazaar style, but it would be very hard to *originate* a project in bazaar mode. Linus didn't try it. I didn't either. Your nascent developer community needs to have something runnable and testable to play with.

When you start community-building, what you need to be able to present is a *plausible promise*. Your program doesn't have to work particularly well. It can be crude, buggy, incomplete, and poorly documented. What it must not fail to do is (a) run, and (b) convince potential co-developers that it can be evolved into something really neat in the foreseeable future.

Linux and fetchmail both went public with strong, attractive basic designs. Many people thinking about the bazaar model as I have presented it have correctly considered this critical, then jumped from that to the conclusion that a high degree of design intuition and cleverness in the project leader is indispensable.

But Linus got his design from Unix. I got mine initially from the ancestral popclient (though it would later change a great deal, much more proportionately speaking than has Linux). So does the leader/coordinator for a bazaar-style effort really have to have exceptional design talent, or can he get by through leveraging the design talent of others?

I think it is not critical that the coordinator be able to originate designs of exceptional brilliance, but it is absolutely critical that the coordinator be able to *recognize good design ideas from others*.

Both the Linux and fetchmail projects show evidence of this. Linus, while not (as previously discussed) a spectacularly original designer, has displayed a powerful knack for recognizing good design and integrating it into the Linux kernel. And I have already described how the single most powerful design idea in fetchmail (SMTP forwarding) came from somebody else.

Early audiences of this essay complimented me by suggesting that I am prone to undervalue design originality in bazaar projects because I have a lot of it myself, and therefore take it for granted. There may be some truth to this; design (as opposed to coding or debugging) is certainly my strongest skill.

But the problem with being clever and original in software design is that it gets to be a habit—you start reflexively making things cute and complicated when you should be keeping them robust and simple. I have had projects crash on me because I made this mistake, but I managed to avoid this with fetchmail.

So I believe the fetchmail project succeeded partly because I restrained my tendency to be clever; this argues (at least) against design originality being essential for successful bazaar projects. And consider Linux. Suppose Linus Torvalds had been trying to pull off fundamental innovations in operating system design during the development; does it seem at all likely that the resulting kernel would be as stable and successful as what we have?

A certain base level of design and coding skill is required, of course, but I expect almost anybody seriously thinking of launching a bazaar effort will already be above that minimum. The open-source community's internal market in reputation exerts subtle pressure on people not to launch development efforts they're not competent to follow through on. So far this seems to have worked pretty well.

There is another kind of skill not normally associated with software development which I think is as important as design cleverness to bazaar projects—and it may be more important. A bazaar project coordinator or leader must have good people and communications skills.

This should be obvious. In order to build a development community, you need to attract people, interest them in what you're doing, and keep them happy about the amount of work they're doing. Technical sizzle will go a long way towards accomplishing this, but it's far from the whole story. The personality you project matters, too.

It is not a coincidence that Linus is a nice guy who makes people like him and want to help him. It's not a coincidence that I'm an energetic extrovert who enjoys working a crowd and has some of the delivery and instincts of a stand-up comic. To make the bazaar model work, it helps enormously if you have at least a little skill at charming people.

THE SOCIAL CONTEXT OF OPEN-SOURCE SOFTWARE

It is truly written: the best hacks start out as personal solutions to the author's everyday problems, and spread because the problem turns out to be typical for a large class of users. This takes us back to the matter of rule 1, restated in a perhaps more useful way:

> 18.TO SOLVE AN INTERESTING PROBLEM, START BY FINDING
> A PROBLEM THAT IS INTERESTING TO YOU.

So it was with Carl Harris and the ancestral popclient, and so with me and fetchmail. But this has been understood for a long time. The interesting point, the point that the histories of Linux and fetchmail seem to demand we focus on, is the next stage—the evolution of software in the presence of a large and active community of users and co-developers.

In *The Mythical Man-Month*, Fred Brooks observed that programmer time is not fungible; adding developers to a late software project makes it later. As we've seen previously, he argued that the complexity and communication costs of a project rise with the square of the number of developers, while work done only rises linearly. Brooks's Law has been widely regarded as a truism. But we've examined in this essay a number of ways in which the process of open-source development falsifies the assumptionms behind it—and, empirically, if Brooks's Law were the whole picture, Linux would be impossible.

Gerald Weinberg's classic *The Psychology of Computer Programming* supplied what, in hindsight, we can see as a vital correction to Brooks. In his discussion of egoless programming, Weinberg observed that in shops where developers are not territorial about their code, and encourage other people to look for bugs and potential improvements in it, improvement happens dramatically faster than elsewhere. (Recently, Kent Beck's 'extreme programming' technique of deploying coders in pairs who look over one another's shoulders might be seen as an attempt to force this effect.)

Weinberg's choice of terminology has perhaps prevented his analysis from gaining the acceptance it deserved—one has to smile at the thought of describing Internet hackers as egoless. But I think his argument looks more compelling today than ever.

The bazaar method, by harnessing the full power of the egoless programming effect, strongly mitigates the effect of Brooks's Law. The principle behind Brooks's Law is not repealed, but given a large developer population and cheap communications its effects can be swamped by competing nonlinearities that are not otherwise visible. This resembles the relationship between Newtonian and Einsteinian physics—the older system is still valid at low energies, but if you push mass and velocity high enough you get surprises like nuclear explosions or Linux.

The history of Unix should have prepared us for what we're learning from Linux (and what I've verified experimentally on a smaller scale by deliberately copying Linus's methods [9]). That is, while coding remains an essentially solitary activity, the really great hacks come from harnessing the attention and brainpower of entire communities. The developer who uses only his or her own brain in a closed project is going to fall behind the developer who knows how to create an open, evolutionary context in which feedback exploring the design space, code contributions, bug-spotting, and other improvements come from from hundreds (perhaps thousands) of people.

But the traditional Unix world was prevented from pushing this approach to the ultimate by several factors. One was the legal contraints of various licenses, trade secrets, and commercial interests. Another (in hindsight) was that the Internet wasn't yet good enough.

Before cheap Internet, there were some geographically compact communities where the culture encouraged Weinberg's egoless programming, and a developer could easily attract a lot of skilled kibitzers and co-developers. Bell Labs, the MIT AI and LCS labs, UC Berkeley—these became the home of innovations that are legendary and still potent.

Linux was the first project for which a conscious and successful effort to use the entire *world* as its talent pool was made. I don't think it's a coincidence that the gestation period of Linux coincided with the birth of the World Wide Web, and that Linux left its infancy during the same period in 1993–1994 that saw the takeoff of the ISP industry and the explosion of mainstream interest in the Internet. Linus was the first person who learned how to play by the new rules that pervasive Internet access made possible.

While cheap Internet was a necessary condition for the Linux model to evolve, I think it was not by itself a sufficient condition. Another vital factor was the development of a leadership style and set of cooperative customs that could allow developers to attract co-developers and get maximum leverage out of the medium.

But what is this leadership style and what are these customs? They cannot be based on power relationships—and even if they could be, leadership by coercion would not produce the results we see.

Weinberg quotes the autobiography of the 19th-century Russian anarchist Pyotr Alexeyvich Kropotkin's *Memoirs of a Revolutionist* to good effect on this subject:

> *Having been brought up in a serf-owner's family, I entered active life, like all young men of my time, with a great deal of confidence in the necessity of commanding, ordering, scolding, punishing and the like. But when, at an early stage, I had to manage serious enterprises and to deal with [free] men, and when each mistake would lead at once to heavy consequences, I began to appreciate the difference between acting on the principle of command and discipline and acting on the principle of common understanding. The former works admirably in a military parade, but it is worth nothing where real life is concerned, and the aim can be achieved only through the severe effort of many converging wills.*

The "severe effort of many converging wills" is precisely what a project like Linux requires—and the "principle of command" is effectively impossible to apply among volunteers in the anarchist's paradise we call the Internet. To operate and compete effectively, hackers who want to lead collaborative projects have to learn how to recruit and energize effective communities of interest in the mode vaguely suggested by Kropotkin's "principle of understanding". They must learn to use Linus's Law [10].

Earlier, I referred to the Delphi Effect as a possible explanation for Linus's Law. But more powerful analogies to adaptive systems in biology and economics also irresistably suggest themselves. The Linux world behaves in many respects like a free market or an ecology, a collection of selfish agents attempting to maximize utility, which in the process produces a self-correcting spontaneous order more elaborate and efficient than any amount of central planning could have achieved. Here, then, is the place to seek the "principle of understanding".

The "utility function" Linux hackers are maximizing is not classically economic, but is the intangible of their own ego satisfaction and reputation among other hackers. (One may call their motivation "altruistic", but this ignores the fact that altruism is itself a form of ego satisfaction for the altruist.) Voluntary cultures that work this way are not actually uncommon; one other in which I have long participated is science fiction fandom, which unlike hackerdom has long explicitly recognized "egoboo" (ego-boosting, or the enhancement of one's reputation among other fans) as the basic drive behind volunteer activity.

Linus, by successfully positioning himself as the gatekeeper of a project in which the development is mostly done by others, and nurturing interest in the project until it became self-sustaining, has shown an acute grasp of Kropotkin's "principle of shared understanding". This quasi-economic view of the Linux world enables us to see how that understanding is applied.

We may view Linus's method as a way to create an efficient market in "egoboo"—to connect the selfishness of individual hackers as firmly as possible to difficult ends that can only be achieved by sustained cooperation. With the fetchmail project I have shown (albeit on a smaller scale) that his methods can be duplicated with good results. Perhaps I have even done it a bit more consciously and systematically than he.

Many people (especially those who politically distrust free markets) would expect a culture of self-directed egoists to be fragmented, territorial, wasteful, secretive, and hostile. But this expectation is clearly falsified by (to give just one example) the stunning variety, quality, and depth of Linux documentation. It is a hallowed given that programmers *hate* documenting; how is it, then, that Linux hackers generate so much documentation? Evidently Linux's free market in egoboo works better to produce virtuous, other-directed behavior than the massively-funded documentation shops of commercial software producers.

Both the fetchmail and Linux kernel projects show that by properly rewarding the egos of many other hackers, a strong developer/coordinator can use the Internet to capture the benefits of having lots of co-developers without having a project collapse into a chaotic mess. So to Brooks's Law, I counter-propose the following:

19.PROVIDED THE DEVELOPMENT COORDINATOR HAS A COMMUNICATIONS MEDIUM AT LEAST AS GOOD AS THE INTERNET, AND KNOWS HOW TO LEAD WITHOUT COERCION, MANY HEADS ARE INEVITABLY BETTER THAN ONE.

I think the future of open-source software will increasingly belong to people who know how to play Linus's game, people who leave behind the cathedral and embrace the bazaar. This is not to say that individual vision and brilliance will no longer matter; rather, I think that the cutting edge of open-source software will belong to people who start from individual vision and brilliance, then amplify it through the effective construction of voluntary communities of interest.

Perhaps this is not only the future of *open-source* software. No closed-source developer can match the pool of talent the Linux community can bring to bear on a problem. Very few could afford even to hire the more than 200 (1999: 600, 2000: 800) people who have contributed to fetchmail!

Perhaps in the end the open-source culture will triumph not because cooperation is morally right or software "hoarding" is morally wrong (assuming you believe the latter, which neither Linus nor I do), but simply because the closed-source world cannot win an evolutionary arms race with open-source communities that can put orders of magnitude more skilled time into a problem.

On Management and the Maginot Line

The original *Cathedral and Bazaar* paper of 1997 ended with the vision above—that of happy networked hordes of programmer/anarchists outcompeting and overwhelming the hierarchical world of conventional closed software.

A good many skeptics weren't convinced, however; and the questions they raise deserve a fair engagement. Most of the objections to the bazaar argument come down to the claim that its proponents have underestimated the productivity-multiplying effect of conventional management.

Traditionally-minded software-development managers often object that the casualness with which project groups form and change and dissolve in the open-source world negates a significant part of the apparent advantage of numbers that the open-source community has over any single closed-source developer. They would observe that in software development it is really sustained effort over time and the degree to which customers can expect continuing investment in the product that matters, not just how many people have thrown a bone in the pot and left it to simmer.

There is something to this argument, to be sure; in fact, I have developed the idea that expected future service value is the key to the economics of software production in the essay *The Magic Cauldron* .

But this argument also has a major hidden problem; its implicit assumption that open-source development cannot deliver such sustained effort. In fact, there have been open-source projects that maintained a coherent direction and an effective maintainer community over quite long periods of time without the kinds of incentive structures or institutional controls that conventional management finds essential. The development of the GNU Emacs editor is an extreme and instructive example; it has absorbed the efforts of hundreds of contributors over 15 years into a unified architectural vision, despite high turnover and the fact that only one person (its author) has been continuously active during all that time. No closed-source editor has ever matched this longevity record.

This suggests a reason for questioning the advantages of conventionally-managed software development that is independent of the rest of the arguments over cathedral versus bazaar mode. If it's possible for GNU Emacs to express a consistent architectural vision over 15 years, or for an operating system like Linux to do the same over 8 years of rapidly changing hardware and platform technology; and if (as is indeed the case) there have been many well-architected open-source projects of more than 5 years duration—then we are entitled to wonder what, if anything, the tremendous overhead of conventionally managed development is actually buying us.

Whatever it is certainly doesn't include reliable execution by deadline, or on budget, or to all features of the specification; it's a rare managed project that meets even one of these goals, let alone all three. It also does not appear to be ability to adapt to changes in technology and economic context during the project lifetime, either; the open-source community has proven *far* more effective on that score (as one can readily verify, for example, by comparing the 30-year history of the Internet with the short half-lives of proprietary networking technologies—or the cost of the 16-bit to 32-bit transition in Microsoft Windows with the nearly effortless upward migration of Linux during the same period, not only along the Intel line of development but to more than a dozen other hardware platforms, including the 64-bit Alpha as well).

One thing many people think the traditional mode buys you is somebody to hold legally liable and potentially recover compensation from if the project goes wrong. But this is an illusion; most software licenses are written to disclaim even warranty of merchantability, let alone performance—and cases of successful recovery for software nonperformance are vanishingly rare. Even if they were common, feeling comforted by having somebody to sue would be missing the point. You didn't want to be in a lawsuit; you wanted working software.

So what is all that management overhead buying?

In order to understand that, we need to understand what software development managers believe they do. A woman I know who seems to be very good at this job says software project management has five functions:

- To *define goals* and keep everybody pointed in the same direction
- To *monitor* and make sure crucial details don't get skipped
- To *motivate* people to do boring but necessary drudgework
- To *organize* the deployment of people for best productivity
- To *marshal resources* needed to sustain the project

Apparently worthy goals, all of these; but under the open-source model, and in its surrounding social context, they can begin to seem strangely irrelevant. We'll take them in reverse order.

My friend reports that a lot of *resource marshalling* is basically defensive; once you have your people and machines and office space, you have to defend them from peer managers competing for the same resources and from higher-ups trying to allocate the most efficient use of a limited pool.

But open-source developers are volunteers, self-selected for both interest and ability to contribute to the projects they work on (and this remains generally true even when they are being paid a salary to hack open source). The volunteer ethos tends to take care of the 'attack' side of resource-marshalling automatically; people bring their own resources to the table. And there is little or no need for a manager to 'play defense' in the conventional sense.

Anyway, in a world of cheap PCs and fast Internet links, we find pretty consistently that the only really limiting resource is skilled attention. Open-source projects, when they founder, essentially never do so for want of machines or links or office space; they die only when the developers themselves lose interest.

That being the case, it's doubly important that open-source hackers *organize themselves* for maximum productivity by self-selection—and the social milieu selects ruthlessly for competence. My friend, familiar with both the open-source world and large closed projects, believes that open source has been successful partly because its culture only accepts the most talented 5% or so of the programming population. She spends most of her time organizing the deployment of the other 95%, and has thus observed first-hand the well-known variance of a factor of one hundred in productivity between the most able programmers and the merely competent.

The size of that variance has always raised an awkward question: would individual projects, and the field as a whole, be better off without more than 50% of the least able in it? Thoughtful managers have understood for a long time that if conventional software management's only function were to convert the least able from a net loss to a marginal win, the game might not be worth the candle.

The success of the open-source community sharpens this question considerably, by providing hard evidence that it is often cheaper and more effective to recruit self-selected volunteers from the Internet than it is to manage buildings full of people who would rather be doing something else.

Which brings us neatly to the question of *motivation*. An equivalent and often-heard way to state my friend's point is that traditional development management is a necessary compensation for poorly motivated programmers who would not otherwise turn out good work.

This answer usually travels with a claim that the open-source community can only be relied on to do work that is "sexy" or technically sweet; anything else will be left undone (or done only poorly) unless it's churned out by money-motivated cubicle peons with managers cracking whips over them. I address the psychological and social reasons for being skeptical of this claim in *Homesteading the Noosphere*. For present purposes, however, I think it's more interesting to point out the implications of accepting it as true.

If the conventional, closed-source, heavily-managed style of software development is really defended only by a sort of Maginot Line of problems conducive to boredom, then it's going to remain viable in each individual application area for only so long as nobody finds those problems really interesting and nobody else finds any way to route around them. Because the moment there is open-source competition for a boring piece of software, customers are going to know that it was finally tackled by someone who chose that problem to solve because of a fascination with the problem itself—which, in software as in other kinds of creative work, is a far more effective motivator than money alone.

Having a conventional management structure solely in order to motivate, then, is probably good tactics but bad strategy; a short-term win, but in the longer term a surer loss.

So far, conventional development management looks like a bad bet now against open source on two points (resource marshalling, organization), and like it's living on borrowed time with respect to a third (motivation). And the poor beleaguered conventional manager is not going to get any succour from the *monitoring* issue; the strongest argument the open-source community has is that decentralized peer review trumps all the conventional methods for trying to ensure that details don't get slipped.

Can we save *defining goals* as a justification for the overhead of conventional software project management? Perhaps; but to do so, we'll need good reason to believe that management committees and corporate roadmaps are more successful at defining worthy and widely shared goals than the project leaders and tribal elders who fill the analogous role in the open-source world.

That is on the face of it a pretty hard case to make. And it's not so much the open-source side of the balance (the longevity of Emacs, or Linus Torvalds's ability to mobilize hordes of developers with talk of world domination) that makes it tough. Rather, it's the demonstrated awfulness of conventional mechanisms for defining the goals of software projects.

One of the best-known folk theorems of software engineering is that 60 to 75% of conventional software projects either are never completed or are rejected by their intended users. If that range is anywhere near true (and I've never met a manager of any experience who disputes it), then more projects than not are being aimed at goals that are either (a) not realistically attainable, or (b) just plain wrong.

This, more than any other problem, is the reason that in today's software engineering world the very phrase "management committee" is likely to send chills down the hearer's spine—even (or perhaps especially) if the hearer is a manager. The days when only programmers griped about this pattern are long past; Dilbert cartoons hang over *executives'* desks now.

Our reply, then, to the traditional software development manager, is simple—if the open-source community has really underestimated the value of conventional management, *why do so many of you display contempt for your own process?*

Once again the example of the open-source community sharpens this question considerably—because we have *fun* doing what we do. Our creative play has been racking up technical, market-share, and mind-share successes at an astounding rate. We're proving not only that we can do better software, but that *joy is an asset.*

Two and a half years after the first version of this essay, the most radical thought I can offer to close with is no longer a vision of an open-source–dominated software world; that, after all, looks plausible to a lot of sober people in suits these days.

Rather, I want to suggest what may be a wider lesson about software (and probably about every kind of creative or professional work). Human beings generally take pleasure in a task when it falls in a sort of optimal-challenge zone; not so easy as to be boring, not too hard to achieve. A happy programmer is one who is neither underutilized nor weighed down with ill-formulated goals and stressful process friction. *Enjoyment predicts efficiency.*

Relating to your own work process with fear and loathing (even in the displaced, ironic way suggested by hanging up Dilbert cartoons) should therefore be regarded in itself as a sign that the process has failed. Joy, humor, and playfulness are indeed assets; it was not mainly for the alliteration that I wrote of "happy hordes" above, and it is no mere joke that the Linux mascot is a cuddly, neotenous penguin.

It may well turn out that one of the most important effects of open source's success will be to teach us that play is the most economically efficient mode of creative work.

EPILOG: NETSCAPE EMBRACES THE BAZAAR

It's a strange feeling to realize you're helping make history . . . .

On 22 January 1998, approximately seven months after I first published *The Cathedral and the Bazaar*, Netscape Communications, Inc. announced plans to give away the source for Netscape Communicator (see *http://www.netscape.com/newsref/pr/newsrelease558.html*). I had had no clue this was going to happen before the day of the announcement.

Eric Hahn, executive vice president and chief technology officer at Netscape, emailed me shortly afterwards as follows: "On behalf of everyone at Netscape, I want to thank you for helping us get to this point in the first place. Your thinking and writings were fundamental inspirations to our decision."

The following week I flew out to Silicon Valley at Netscape's invitation for a day-long strategy conference (on 4 February 1998) with some of their top executives and technical people. We designed Netscape's source-release strategy and license together.

A few days later I wrote the following:

> Netscape is about to provide us with a large-scale, real-world test of the bazaar model in the commercial world. The open-source culture now faces a danger; if Netscape's execution doesn't work, the open-source concept may be so discredited that the commercial world won't touch it again for another decade.
>
> On the other hand, this is also a spectacular opportunity. Initial reaction to the move on Wall Street and elsewhere has been cautiously positive. We're being given a chance to prove ourselves, too. If Netscape regains substantial market share through this move, it just may set off a long-overdue revolution in the software industry.
>
> The next year should be a very instructive and interesting time.

And indeed it was. As I write in mid-2000, the development of what was later named Mozilla has been only a qualified success. It achieved Netscape's original goal, which was to deny Microsoft a monopoly lock on the browser market. It has also achieved some dramatic successes (notably the release of the next-generation Gecko rendering engine).

However, it has not yet garnered the massive development effort from outside Netscape that the Mozilla founders had originally hoped for. The problem here seems to be that for a long time the Mozilla distribution actually broke one of the basic rules of the bazaar model; it didn't ship with something potential contributors could easily run and see working. (Until more than a year after release, building Mozilla from source required a license for the proprietary Motif library.)

Most negatively (from the point of view of the outside world) the Mozilla group didn't ship a production-quality browser for two and a half years after the project launch—and in 1999 one of the project's principals caused a bit of a sensation by resigning, complaining of poor management and missed opportunities. "Open source," he correctly observed, "is not magic pixie dust."

And indeed it is not. The long-term prognosis for Mozilla looks dramatically better now (in November 2000) than it did at the time of Jamie Zawinski's resignation letter—in the last few weeks the nightly releases have finally passed the critical threshold to production usability. But Jamie was right to point out that going open will not necessarily save an existing project that suffers from ill-defined goals or spaghetti code or any of the software engineering's other chronic ills. Mozilla has managed to provide an example simultaneously of how open source can succeed and how it could fail.

In the mean time, however, the open-source idea has scored successes and found backers elsewhere. Since the Netscape release we've seen a tremendous explosion of interest in the open-source development model, a trend both driven by and driving the continuing success of the Linux operating system. The trend Mozilla touched off is continuing at an accelerating rate.

HOMESTEADING THE NOOSPHERE

✦ ✦ ✦

After observing a contradiction between the official ideology defined by open-source licenses and the actual behavior of hackers, I examine the actual customs that regulate the ownership and control of open-source software. I show that they imply an underlying theory of property rights homologous to the Lockean theory of land tenure. I then relate that to an analysis of the hacker culture as a 'gift culture' in which participants compete for prestige by giving time, energy, and creativity away. Finally, I examine the consequences of this analysis for conflict resolution in the culture, and develop some prescriptive implications.

AN INTRODUCTORY CONTRADICTION

Anyone who watches the busy, tremendously productive world of Internet open-source software for a while is bound to notice an interesting contradiction between what open-source hackers say they believe and the way they actually behave—between the official ideology of the open-source culture and its actual practice.

Cultures are adaptive machines. The open-source culture is a response to an identifiable set of drives and pressures. As usual, the culture's adaptation to its circumstances manifests both as conscious ideology and as implicit, unconscious or semi-conscious knowledge. And, as is not uncommon, the unconscious adaptations are partly at odds with the conscious ideology.

In this essay, I will dig around the roots of that contradiction, and use it to discover those drives and pressures. I will deduce some interesting things about the hacker culture and its customs. I will conclude by suggesting ways in which the culture's implicit knowledge can be leveraged better.

THE VARIETIES OF HACKER IDEOLOGY

The ideology of the Internet open-source culture (what hackers say they believe) is a fairly complex topic in itself. All members agree that open source (that is, software that is freely redistributable and can readily evolve and be modified to fit changing needs) is a good thing and worthy of significant and collective effort. This agreement effectively defines membership in the culture. However, the reasons individuals and various subcultures give for this belief vary considerably.

One degree of variation is zealotry; whether open source development is regarded merely as a convenient means to an end (good tools and fun toys and an interesting game to play) or as an end in itself.

A person of great zeal might say, "Free software is my life! I exist to create useful, beautiful programs and information resources, and then give them away." A person of moderate zeal might say, "Open source is a good thing, which I am willing to spend significant time helping happen." A person of little zeal might say, "Yes, open source is okay sometimes. I play with it and respect people who build it."

Another degree of variation is in hostility to commercial software and/or the companies perceived to dominate the commercial software market.

A very anticommercial person might say, "Commercial software is theft and hoarding. I write free software to end this evil." A moderately anticommercial person might say, "Commercial software in general is okay because programmers deserve to get paid, but companies that coast on shoddy products and throw their weight around are evil." An un-anticommercial person might say, "Commercial software is okay; I just use and/or write open-source software because I like it better." (Nowadays, given the growth of the open-source part of the industry since the first public version of this essay, one might also hear, "Commercial software is fine, as long as I get the source or it does what I want it to do.")

All nine of the attitudes implied by the cross-product of the categories mentioned earlier are represented in the open-source culture. It is worthwhile to point out the distinctions because they imply different agendas and different adaptive and cooperative behaviors.

Historically, the most visible and best-organized part of the hacker culture has been both very zealous and very anticommercial. The Free Software Foundation founded by Richard M. Stallman

(RMS) supported a great deal of open-source development from the early 1980s forward, including tools like Emacs and GCC, which are still basic to the Internet open-source world, and seem likely to remain so for the forseeable future.

For many years the FSF was the single most important focus of open-source hacking, producing a huge number of tools still critical to the culture. The FSF was also long the only sponsor of open source with an institutional identity visible to outside observers of the hacker culture. They effectively defined the term 'free software', deliberately giving it a confrontational weight (which the newer label 'open source' [*http://www.opensource.org*] just as deliberately avoids).

Thus, perceptions of the hacker culture from both within and without it tended to identify the culture with the FSF's zealous attitude and perceived anticommercial aims. RMS himself denies he is anticommercial, but his program has been so read by most people, including many of his most vocal partisans. The FSF's vigorous and explicit drive to "Stamp Out Software Hoarding!" became the closest thing to a hacker ideology, and RMS the closest thing to a leader of the hacker culture.

The FSF's license terms, the "General Public License" (GPL), expresses the FSF's attitudes. It is very widely used in the open-source world. North Carolina's Metalab (*http://metalab.unc.edu/pub/Linux/welcome.html*; formerly Sunsite) is the largest and most popular software archive in the Linux world. In July 1997 about half the Sunsite software packages with explicit license terms used GPL.

But the FSF was never the only game in town. There was always a quieter, less confrontational and more market-friendly strain in the hacker culture. The pragmatists were loyal not so much to an ideology as to a group of engineering traditions founded on early open-source efforts that predated the FSF. These traditions included, most importantly, the intertwined technical cultures of Unix and the pre-commercial Internet.

The typical pragmatist attitude is only moderately anticommercial, and its major grievance against the corporate world is not 'hoarding' *per se*. Rather it is that world's perverse refusal to adopt superior approaches incorporating Unix and open standards and open-source software. If the pragmatist hates anything, it is less likely to be 'hoarders' in general than the current King Log of the software establishment; formerly IBM, now Microsoft.

To pragmatists the GPL is important as a tool, rather than as an end in itself. Its main value is not as a weapon against hoarding, but as a tool for encouraging software sharing and the growth of bazaar-mode development communities. The pragmatist values having good tools and toys more than he dislikes commercialism, and may use high-quality commercial software without ideological discomfort. At the same time, his open-source experience has taught him standards of technical quality that very little closed software can meet.

For many years, the pragmatist point of view expressed itself within the hacker culture mainly as a stubborn current of refusal to completely buy into the GPL in particular or the FSF's agenda in general. Through the 1980s and early 1990s, this attitude tended to be associated with fans of Berkeley Unix, users of the BSD license, and the early efforts to build open-source Unixes from the BSD source base. These efforts, however, failed to build bazaar communities of significant size, and became seriously fragmented and ineffective.

Not until the Linux explosion of early 1993–1994 did pragmatism find a real power base. Although Linus Torvalds never made a point of opposing RMS, he set an example by looking benignly on the growth of a commercial Linux industry, by publicly endorsing the use of high-quality commercial software for specific tasks, and by gently deriding the more purist and fanatical elements in the culture.

A side effect of the rapid growth of Linux was the induction of a large number of new hackers for which Linux was their primary loyalty and the FSF's agenda primarily of historical interest. Though the newer wave of Linux hackers might describe the system as "the choice of a GNU generation", most tended to emulate Torvalds more than Stallman.

Increasingly it was the anticommercial purists who found themselves in a minority. How much things had changed would not become apparent until the Netscape announcement in February 1998 that it would distribute Navigator 5.0 in source. This excited more interest in 'free software' within the corporate world. The subsequent call to the hacker culture to exploit this unprecedented opportunity and to re-label its product from 'free software' to 'open source' was met with a level of instant approval that surprised everybody involved.

In a reinforcing development, the pragmatist part of the culture was itself becoming polycentric by the mid-1990s. Other semi-independent communities with their own self-consciousness and charismatic leaders began to bud from the Unix/Internet root stock. Of these, the most important after Linux was the Perl culture under Larry Wall. Smaller, but still significant, were the traditions building up around John Osterhout's Tcl and Guido van Rossum's Python languages. All three of these communities expressed their ideological independence by devising their own, non-GPL licensing schemes.

Promiscuous Theory, Puritan Practice

Through all these changes, nevertheless, there remained a broad consensus theory of what 'free software' or 'open source' is. The clearest expression of this common theory can be found in the various open-source licenses, all of which have crucial common elements.

In 1997 these common elements were distilled into the Debian Free Software Guidelines, which became the Open Source Definition (*http://www.opensource.org*). Under the guidelines defined by the OSD, an open-source license must protect an unconditional right of any party to modify (and redistribute modified versions of) open-source software.

Thus, the implicit theory of the OSD (and OSD-conformant licenses such as the GPL, the BSD license, and Perl's Artistic License) is that anyone can hack anything. Nothing prevents half a dozen different people from taking any given open-source product (such as, say the Free Software Foundations's gcc C compiler), duplicating the sources, running off with them in different evolutionary directions, but all claiming to be *the* product.

This kind of divergence is called a *fork*. The most important characteristic of a fork is that it spawns competing projects that cannot later exchange code, splitting the potential developer community. (There are phenomena that look superficially like forking but are not, such as the proliferation of different Linux distributions. In these pseudo-forking cases there may be separate projects, but they use mostly common code and can benefit from each other's development efforts completely enough that they are neither technically nor sociologically a waste, and are not perceived as forks.)

The open-source licenses do nothing to restrain forking, let alone pseudo-forking; in fact, one could argue that they implicitly encourage both. In practice, however, pseudo-forking is common but forking almost never happens. Splits in major projects have been rare, and are always accompanied by re-labeling and a large volume of public self-justification. It is clear, in such cases as the GNU Emacs/XEmacs split, or the gcc/egcs split, or the various fissionings of the BSD splinter groups, that the splitters felt they were going against a fairly powerful community norm [1].

In fact (and in contradiction to the anyone-can-hack-anything consensus theory) the open-source culture has an elaborate but largely unadmitted set of ownership customs.

These customs regulate who can modify software, the circumstances under which it can be modified, and (especially) who has the right to redistribute modified versions back to the community.

The taboos of a culture throw its norms into sharp relief. Therefore, it will be useful later on if we summarize some important ones here:

- There is strong social pressure against forking projects. It does not happen except under plea of dire necessity, with much public self-justification, and requires renaming.

- Distributing changes to a project without the cooperation of the moderators is frowned upon, except in special cases like essentially trivial porting fixes.

- Removing a person's name from a project history, credits, or maintainer list is absolutely *not done* without the person's explicit consent.

In the remainder of this essay, we shall examine these taboos and ownership customs in detail. We shall inquire not only into how they function but what they reveal about the underlying social dynamics and incentive structures of the open-source community.

OWNERSHIP AND OPEN SOURCE

What does 'ownership' mean when property is infinitely reduplicable, highly malleable, and the surrounding culture has neither coercive power relationships nor material scarcity economics?

Actually, in the case of the open-source culture this is an easy question to answer. The owner of a software project is the person who has the exclusive right, recognized by the community at large, to *distribute modified versions*.

(In discussing 'ownership' in this section I will use the singular, as though all projects are owned by some one person. It should be understood, however, that projects may be owned by groups. We shall examine the internal dynamics of such groups later on.)

According to the standard open-source licenses, all parties are equals in the evolutionary game. But in practice there is a very well-recognized distinction between 'official' patches, approved and integrated into the evolving software by the publicly recognized maintainers, and 'rogue' patches by third parties. Rogue patches are unusual, and generally not trusted [2].

That *public* redistribution is the fundamental issue is easy to establish. Custom encourages people to patch software for personal use when necessary. Custom is indifferent to people who redistribute modified versions within a closed user or development group. It is only when modifications are posted to the open-source community in general, to compete with the original, that ownership becomes an issue.

There are, in general, three ways to acquire ownership of an open-source project. One, the most obvious, is to found the project. When a project has had only one maintainer since its inception and the maintainer is still active, custom does not even permit a *question* as to who owns the project.

The second way is to have ownership of the project handed to you by the previous owner (this is sometimes known as "passing the baton"). It is well understood in the community that project owners have a duty to pass projects to competent successors when they are no longer willing or able to invest needed time in development or maintenance work.

It is significant that in the case of major projects, such transfers of control are generally announced with some fanfare. While it is unheard of for the open-source community at large to actually interfere in the owner's choice of succession, customary practice clearly incorporates a premise that public legitimacy is important.

For minor projects, it is generally sufficient for a change history included with the project distribution to note the change of ownership. The clear presumption is that if the former owner has not in fact voluntarily transferred control, he or she may reassert control with community backing by objecting publicly within a reasonable period of time.

The third way to acquire ownership of a project is to observe that it needs work and the owner has disappeared or lost interest. If you want to do this, it is your responsibility to make the effort to find the owner. If you don't succeed, then you may announce in a relevant place (such as a Usenet newsgroup dedicated to the application area) that the project appears to be orphaned, and that you are considering taking responsibility for it.

Custom demands that you allow some time to pass before following up with an announcement that you have declared yourself the new owner. In this interval, if someone else announces that they have been actually working on the project, their claim trumps yours. It is considered good form to give public notice of your intentions more than once. You get more points for good form if you announce in many relevant forums (related newsgroups, mailing lists), and still more if you show patience in waiting for replies. In general, the more visible effort you make to allow the previous owner or other claimants to respond, the better your claim if no response is forthcoming.

If you have gone through this process in sight of the project's user community, and there are no objections, then you may claim ownership of the orphaned project and so note in its history file. This, however, is less secure than being passed the baton, and you cannot expect to be considered fully legitimate until you have made substantial improvements in the sight of the user community.

I have observed these customs in action for 20 years, going back to the pre-FSF ancient history of open-source software. They have several very interesting features. One of the most interesting is that most hackers have followed them without being fully aware of doing so. Indeed, this may be the first conscious and reasonably complete summary ever to have been written down.

Another is that, for unconscious customs, they have been followed with remarkable (even astonishing) consistency. I have observed the evolution of literally hundreds of open-source projects, and I can still count the number of significant violations I have observed or heard about on my fingers.

Yet a third interesting feature is that as these customs have evolved over time, they have done so in a consistent direction. That direction has been to encourage more public accountability, more public notice, and more care about preserving the credits and change histories of projects in ways that (among other things) establish the legitimacy of the present owners.

These features suggest that the customs are not accidental, but are products of some kind of implicit agenda or generative pattern in the open-source culture that is utterly fundamental to the way it operates.

An early respondent pointed out that contrasting the Internet hacker culture with the cracker/pirate culture (the "warez d00dz" centered around game-cracking and pirate bulletin-board systems) illuminates the generative patterns of both rather well. We'll return to the d00dz for contrast later in this essay.

LOCKE AND LAND TITLE

To understand this generative pattern, it helps to notice a historical analogy for these customs that is far outside the domain of hackers' usual concerns. As students of legal history and political philosophy may recognize, the theory of property they imply is virtually identical to the Anglo-American common-law theory of land tenure!

In this theory, there are three ways to acquire ownership of land:

On a frontier, where land exists that has never had an owner, one can acquire ownership by *homesteading*, mixing one's labor with the unowned land, fencing it, and defending one's title.

The usual means of transfer in settled areas is *transfer of title*— that is, receiving the deed from the previous owner. In this theory, the concept of 'chain of title' is important. The ideal proof of ownership is a chain of deeds and transfers extending back to when the land was originally homesteaded.

Finally, the common-law theory recognizes that land title may be lost or abandoned (for example, if the owner dies without heirs, or the records needed to establish chain of title to vacant land are gone). A piece of land that has become derelict in this way may be claimed by *adverse possession*—one moves in, improves it, and defends title as if homesteading.

This theory, like hacker customs, evolved organically in a context where central authority was weak or nonexistent. It developed over a period of a thousand years from Norse and Germanic tribal law. Because it was systematized and rationalized in the early modern era by the English political philosopher John Locke, it is sometimes referred to as the Lockean theory of property.

Logically similar theories have tended to evolve wherever property has high economic or survival value and no single authority is powerful enough to force central allocation of scarce goods. This is true even in the hunter-gatherer cultures that are sometimes romantically thought to have no concept of 'property'. For example, in the traditions of the !Kung San bushmen of the Kgalagadi (formerly Kalahari) Desert, there is no ownership of hunting grounds. But there *is* ownership of waterholes and springs under a theory recognizably akin to Locke's.

The !Kung San example is instructive, because it shows that Lockean property customs arise only where the expected return from the resource exceeds the expected cost of defending it. Hunting grounds are not property because the return from hunting is highly unpredictable and variable, and (although highly prized) not a necessity for day-to-day survival. Waterholes, on the other hand, are vital to survival and small enough to defend.

The 'noosphere' of this essay's title is the territory of ideas, the space of all possible thoughts [3]. What we see implied in hacker ownership customs is a Lockean theory of property rights in one subset of the noosphere, the space of all programs. Hence 'homesteading the noosphere', which is what every founder of a new open-source project does.

Faré Rideau (*fare@tunes.org*) correctly points out that hackers do not exactly operate in the territory of pure ideas. He asserts that what hackers own is *programming projects*—intensional focus points of material labor (development, service, etc.), to which are associated things like reputation, trustworthiness, etc. He therefore asserts that the space spanned by hacker projects is *not* the noosphere but a sort of dual of it, the space of noosphere-exploring program projects. (With an apologetic nod to the astrophysicists out there, it would be etymologically correct to call this dual space the 'ergosphere' or 'sphere of work'.)

In practice, the distinction between noosphere and ergosphere is not important for the purposes of our present argument. It is dubious whether the noosphere in the pure sense on which Faré insists can be said to exist in any meaningful way; one would almost have to be a Platonic philosopher to believe in it. And the distinction between noosphere and ergosphere is only of *practical* importance if one wishes to assert that ideas (the elements of the noosphere) cannot be owned, but their instantiations as projects can. This question leads to issues in the theory of intellectual property that are beyond the scope of this essay[4]).

To avoid confusion, however, it is important to note that neither the noosphere nor the ergosphere is the same as the totality of virtual locations in electronic media that is sometimes (to the disgust of most hackers) called 'cyberspace'. Property there is regulated by completely different rules that are closer to those of the material substratum—essentially, he who owns the media and machines on which a part of cyberspace is hosted owns that piece of cyberspace as a result.

The Lockean logic of custom suggests strongly that open-source hackers observe the customs they do in order to defend some kind of expected return from their effort. The return must be more significant than the effort of homesteading projects, the cost of maintaining version histories that document 'chain of title', and the time cost of making public notifications and waiting before taking adverse possession of an orphaned project.

Furthermore, the 'yield' from open source must be something more than simply the use of the software, something else that would be compromised or diluted by forking. If use were the only issue, there would be no taboo against forking, and open-source ownership would not resemble land tenure at all. In fact, this alternate world (where use is the only yield, and forking is unproblematic) is the one implied by existing open-source licenses.

We can eliminate some candidate kinds of yield right away. Because you can't coerce effectively over a network connection, seeking power is right out. Likewise, the open-source culture doesn't have anything much resembling money or an internal scarcity economy, so hackers cannot be pursuing anything very closely analogous to material wealth (e.g., the accumulation of scarcity tokens).

There is one way that open-source activity can help people become wealthier, however—a way that provides a valuable clue to what actually motivates it. Occasionally, the reputation one gains in the hacker culture can spill over into the real world in economically significant ways. It can get you a better job offer, or a consulting contract, or a book deal.

This kind of side effect, however, is at best rare and marginal for most hackers; far too much so to make it convincing as a sole explanation, even if we ignore the repeated protestations by hackers that they're doing what they do not for money but out of idealism or love.

However, the way such economic side effects are mediated is worth examination. Next we'll see that an understanding of the dynamics of reputation within the open-source culture *itself* has considerable explanatory power.

THE HACKER MILIEU AS GIFT CULTURE

To understand the role of reputation in the open-source culture, it is helpful to move from history further into anthropology and economics, and examine the difference between *exchange cultures* and *gift cultures*.

Human beings have an innate drive to compete for social status; it's wired in by our evolutionary history. For the 90% of hominid history that ran before the invention of agriculture, our ancestors lived in small nomadic hunter-gatherer bands. High-status individuals (those most effective at informing coalitions and persuading others to cooperate with them) got the healthiest mates and access to the best food. This drive for status expresses itself in different ways, depending largely on the degree of scarcity of survival goods.

Most ways humans have of organizing are adaptations to scarcity and want. Each way carries with it different ways of gaining social status.

The simplest way is the *command hierarchy*. In command hierarchies, scarce goods are allocated by one central authority and backed up by force. Command hierarchies scale very poorly [5]; they become increasingly brutal and inefficient as they get larger. For this reason, command hierarchies above the size of an extended family are almost always parasites on a larger economy of a different type. In command hierarchies, social status is primarily determined by access to coercive power.

Our society is predominantly an *exchange economy*. This is a sophisticated adaptation to scarcity that, unlike the command model, scales quite well. Allocation of scarce goods is done in a decentralized way through trade and voluntary cooperation (and in fact, the dominating effect of competitive desire is to produce cooperative behavior). In an exchange economy, social status is primarily determined by having control of things (not necessarily material things) to use or trade.

Most people have implicit mental models of both and understand how they interact with each other. Government, the military, and organized crime (for example) are command hierarchies parasitic on the broader exchange economy we call 'the free market'. There's a third model, however, that is radically different from either and not generally recognized except by anthropologists; the *gift culture*.

Gift cultures are adaptations not to scarcity but to abundance. They arise in populations that do not have significant material-scarcity problems with survival goods. We can observe gift cultures in action among aboriginal cultures living in ecozones with mild climates and abundant food. We can also observe them in certain strata of our own society, especially in show business and among the very wealthy.

Abundance makes command relationships difficult to sustain and exchange relationships an almost pointless game. In gift cultures, social status is determined not by what you control but by *what you give away*.

Thus the Kwakiutl chieftain's potlach party. Thus the multi-millionaire's elaborate and usually public acts of philanthropy. And thus the hacker's long hours of effort to produce high-quality open-source code.

For examined in this way, it is quite clear that the society of open-source hackers is in fact a gift culture. Within it, there is no serious shortage of the 'survival necessities'—disk space, network bandwidth, computing power. Software is freely shared. This abundance creates a situation in which the only available measure of competitive success is reputation among one's peers.

This observation is not in itself entirely sufficient to explain the observed features of hacker culture, however. The crackers and warez d00dz have a gift culture that thrives in the same (electronic) media as that of the hackers, but their behavior is very different. The group mentality in their culture is much stronger and more exclusive than among hackers. They hoard secrets rather than sharing them; one is much more likely to find cracker groups distributing sourceless executables that crack software than tips that give away how they did it. (For an inside perspective on this behavior, see endnote 5).

What this shows, in case it wasn't obvious, is that there is more than one way to run a gift culture. History and values matter. I have summarized the history of the hacker culture in *A Brief History of Hackerdom*; the ways in which it shaped present behavior are not mysterious. Hackers have defined their culture by a set of choices about the *form* that their competition will take. It is that form that we will examine in the remainder of this essay.

THE JOY OF HACKING

In making this 'reputation game' analysis, by the way, I do not mean to devalue or ignore the pure artistic satisfaction of designing beautiful software and making it work. Hackers all experience this kind of satisfaction and thrive on it. People for whom it is not a significant motivation never become hackers in the first place, just as people who don't love music never become composers.

So perhaps we should consider another model of hacker behavior in which the pure joy of craftsmanship is the primary motivation. This 'craftsmanship' model would have to explain hacker custom as a way of maximizing both the opportunities for craftsmanship and the quality of the results. Does this conflict with or suggest different results than the reputation game model?

Not really. In examining the craftsmanship model, we come back to the same problems that constrain hackerdom to operate like a gift culture. How can one maximize quality if there is no metric for quality? If scarcity economics doesn't operate, what metrics are available besides peer evaluation? It appears that any craftsmanship culture ultimately must structure itself through a reputation game—and, in fact, we can observe exactly this dynamic in many historical craftsmanship cultures from the medieval guilds onwards.

In one important respect, the craftsmanship model is weaker than the gift culture model; by itself, it doesn't help explain the contradiction we began this essay with.

Finally, the craftsmanship motivation itself may not be psychologically as far removed from the reputation game as we might like to assume. Imagine your beautiful program locked up in a drawer and never used again. Now imagine it being used effectively and with pleasure by many people. Which dream gives you satisfaction?

Nevertheless, we'll keep an eye on the craftsmanship model. It is intuitively appealing to many hackers, and explains some aspects of individual behavior well enough [6].

After I published the first version of this essay on the Internet, an anonymous respondent commented: "You may not work to get reputation, but the reputation is a real payment with consequences if you do the job well." This is a subtle and important point. The reputation incentives continue to operate whether or not a craftsman is aware of them; thus, ultimately, whether or not a hacker understands his own behavior as part of the reputation game, his behavior will be shaped by that game.

Other respondents related peer-esteem rewards and the joy of hacking to the levels above subsistence needs in Abraham Maslow's well-known 'hierarchy of values' model of human motivation [7]. On this view, the joy of hacking fulfills a self-actualization or transcendence need, which will not be consistently expressed until lower-level needs (including those for physical security and for 'belongingness' or peer esteem) have been at least minimally satisfied. Thus, the reputation game may be critical in providing a social context within which the joy of hacking can in fact *become* the individual's primary motive.

THE MANY FACES OF REPUTATION

There are reasons general to every gift culture why peer repute (prestige) is worth playing for:

First and most obviously, good reputation among one's peers is a primary reward. We're wired to experience it that way for evolutionary reasons touched on earlier. (Many people learn to redirect their drive for prestige into various sublimations that have no obvious connection to a visible peer group, such as 'honor', 'ethical integrity', 'piety', etc.; this does not change the underlying mechanism.)

Second, prestige is a good way (and in a pure gift economy, the *only* way) to attract attention and cooperation from others. If one is well known for generosity, intelligence, fair dealing, leadership ability, or other good qualities, it becomes much easier to persuade other people that they will gain by association with you.

Third, if your gift economy is in contact with or intertwined with an exchange economy or a command hierarchy, your reputation may spill over and earn you higher status there.

Beyond these general reasons, the peculiar conditions of the hacker culture make prestige even more valuable than it would be in a 'real world' gift culture.

The main 'peculiar condition' is that the artifacts one gives away (or, interpreted another way, are the visible sign of one's gift of energy and time) are very complex. Their value is nowhere near as obvious as that of material gifts or exchange-economy money. It is much harder to objectively distinguish a fine gift from a poor one. Accordingly, the success of a giver's bid for status is delicately dependent on the critical judgement of peers.

Another peculiarity is the relative purity of the open-source culture. Most gift cultures are compromised—either by exchange-economy relationships such as trade in luxury goods, or by command-economy relationships such as family or clan groupings. No significant analogues of these exist in the open-source culture; thus, ways of gaining status other than by peer repute are virtually absent.

OWNERSHIP RIGHTS AND REPUTATION INCENTIVES

We are now in a position to pull together the previous analyses into a coherent account of hacker ownership customs. We understand the yield from homesteading the noosphere now; it is peer repute in the gift culture of hackers, with all the secondary gains and side effects that implies.

From this understanding, we can analyze the Lockean property customs of hackerdom as a means of *maximizing reputation incentives*—of ensuring that peer credit goes where it is due and does not go where it is not due.

The three taboos we have observed make perfect sense under this analysis. One's reputation can suffer unfairly if someone else misappropriates or mangles one's work; these taboos (and related customs) attempt to prevent this from happening. (Or, to put it more pragmatically, hackers generally refrain from forking or rogue-patching others' projects in order to be able to deny legitimacy to the same behavior practiced against themselves.)

- Forking projects is bad because it exposes pre-fork contributors to a reputation risk they can only control by being active in both child projects simultaneously after the fork. (This would generally be too confusing or difficult to be practical.)

- Distributing rogue patches (or, much worse, rogue binaries) exposes the owners to an unfair reputation risk. Even if the official code is perfect, the owners will catch flak from bugs in the patches (but see endnote 4.).

- Surreptitiously filing someone's name off a project is, in cultural context, one of the ultimate crimes. Doing this steals the victim's gift to be presented as the thief's own.

Of course, forking a project or distributing rogue patches for it also directly attacks the reputation of the original developer's group. If I fork or rogue-patch your project, I am saying, "You made a wrong decision by failing to take the project where I am taking it"; and anyone who uses my forked variation is endorsing this challenge. But this in itself would be a fair challenge, albeit extreme; it's the sharpest end of peer review. It's therefore not sufficient in itself to account for the taboos, though it doubtless contributes force to them.

All three taboo behaviors inflict global harm on the open-source community as well as local harm on the victim(s). Implicitly they damage the entire community by decreasing each potential contributor's perceived likelihood that gift/productive behavior will be rewarded.

It's important to note that there are alternate candidate explanations for two of these three taboos.

First, hackers often explain their antipathy to forking projects by bemoaning the wasteful duplication of work it would imply as the child products evolve on more-or-less parallel courses into the future. They may also observe that forking tends to split the co-developer community, leaving both child projects with fewer brains to use than the parent.

A respondent has pointed out that it is unusual for more than one offspring of a fork to survive with significant 'market share' into the long term. This strengthens the incentives for all parties to cooperate and avoid forking, because it's hard to know in advance who will be on the losing side and see a lot of their work either disappear entirely or languish in obscurity.

It has also been pointed out that the simple fact that forks are likely to produce contention and dispute is enough to motivate social pressure against them. Contention and dispute disrupt the teamwork that is necessary for each individual contributor to reach his or her goals.

Dislike of rogue patches is often explained by the objection that they can create compatibility problems between the daughter versions, complicate bug-tracking enormously, and inflict work on maintainers who have quite enough to do catching their *own* mistakes.

There is considerable truth to these explanations, and they certainly do their bit to reinforce the Lockean logic of ownership. But while intellectually attractive, they fail to explain why so much emotion and territoriality gets displayed on the infrequent occasions that the taboos get bent or broken—not just by the injured parties, but by bystanders and observers who often react quite harshly. Cold-blooded concerns about duplication of work and maintainance hassles simply do not sufficiently explain the observed behavior.

Then, too, there is the third taboo. It's hard to see how anything but the reputation-game analysis can explain this. The fact that this taboo is seldom analyzed much more deeply than "It wouldn't be fair" is revealing in its own way, as we shall see in the next section.

THE PROBLEM OF EGO

At the beginning of this essay I mentioned that the unconscious adaptive knowledge of a culture is often at odds with its conscious ideology. One major example of this is the fact that Lockean ownership customs have been widely followed despite the fact that they violate the stated intent of the standard licenses.

I have observed another interesting example of this phenomenon when discussing the reputation-game analysis with hackers. This is that many hackers resisted the analysis and showed a strong reluctance to admit that their behavior was motivated by a desire for peer repute or, as I incautiously labeled it at the time, 'ego satisfaction'.

This illustrates an interesting point about the hacker culture. It consciously distrusts and despises egotism and ego-based motivations; self-promotion tends to be mercilessly criticized, even when the community might appear to have something to gain from it. So much so, in fact, that the culture's 'big men' and tribal elders are required to talk softly and humorously deprecate themselves at every turn in order to maintain their status. How this attitude meshes with an incentive structure that apparently runs almost entirely on ego cries out for explanation.

A large part of it, certainly, stems from the generally negative Europo-American attitude towards 'ego'. The cultural matrix of most hackers teaches them that desiring ego satisfaction is a bad (or at least immature) motivation; that ego is at best an eccentricity tolerable only in prima donnas and often an actual sign of mental pathology. Only sublimated and disguised forms like 'peer repute', 'self-esteem', 'professionalism', or 'pride of accomplishment' are generally acceptable.

I could write an entire other essay on the unhealthy roots of this part of our cultural inheritance, and the astonishing amount of self-deceptive harm we do by believing (against all the evidence of psychology and behavior) that we ever have truly 'selfless' motives. Perhaps I would, if Friedrich Wilhelm Nietzsche and Ayn Rand had not already done an entirely competent job (whatever their other failings) of deconstructing 'altruism' into unacknowledged kinds of self-interest.

But I am not doing moral philosophy or psychology here, so I will simply observe one minor kind of harm done by the belief that ego is evil, which is this: it has made it emotionally difficult for many hackers to consciously understand the social dynamics of their own culture!

But we are not quite done with this line of investigation. The surrounding culture's taboo against visibly ego-driven behavior is so much intensified in the hacker (sub)culture that one must suspect it of having some sort of special adaptive function for hackers. Certainly the taboo is weaker (or nonexistent) among many other gift cultures, such as the peer cultures of theater people or the very wealthy.

THE VALUE OF HUMILITY

Having established that prestige is central to the hacker culture's reward mechanisms, we now need to understand why it has seemed so important that this fact remain semi-covert and largely unadmitted.

The contrast with the pirate culture is instructive. In that culture, status-seeking behavior is overt and even blatant. These crackers seek acclaim for releasing "zero-day warez" (cracked software redistributed on the day of the original uncracked version's release) but are closemouthed about how they do it. These magicians don't like to give away their tricks. And, as a result, the knowledge base of the cracker culture as a whole increases only slowly.

In the hacker community, by contrast, one's work is one's statement. There's a very strict meritocracy (the best craftsmanship wins) and there's a strong ethos that quality should (indeed *must*) be left to speak for itself. The best brag is code that "just works", and that any competent programmer can see is good stuff. Thus, the hacker culture's knowledge base increases rapidly.

The taboo against ego-driven posturing therefore increases productivity. But that's a second-order effect; what is being directly protected here is the quality of the information in the community's peer-evaluation system. That is, boasting or self-importance is suppressed because it behaves like noise tending to corrupt the vital signals from experiments in creative and cooperative behavior.

For very similar reasons, attacking the author rather than the code is not done. There is an interesting subtlety here that reinforces the point; hackers feel very free to flame each other over ideological and personal differences, but it is unheard of for any hacker to publicly attack another's competence at technical work (even private criticism is unusual and tends to be muted in tone). Bug-hunting and criticism are always project-labeled, not person-labeled.

Furthermore, past bugs are not automatically held against a developer; the fact that a bug has been fixed is generally considered more important than the fact that one used to be there. As one respondent observed, one can gain status by fixing 'Emacs bugs', but not by fixing 'Richard Stallman's bugs'—and it would be considered extremely bad form to criticize Stallman for *old* Emacs bugs that have since been fixed.

This makes an interesting contrast with many parts of academia, in which trashing putatively defective work by others is an important mode of gaining reputation. In the hacker culture, such behavior is rather heavily tabooed—so heavily, in fact, that the absence of such behavior did not present itself to me as a datum until that one respondent with an unusual perspective pointed it out nearly a full year after this essay was first published!

The taboo against attacks on competence (not shared with academia) is even more revealing than the (shared) taboo on posturing, because we can relate it to a difference between academia and hackerdom in their communications and support structures.

The hacker culture's medium of gifting is intangible, its communications channels are poor at expressing emotional nuance, and face-to-face contact among its members is the exception rather than the rule. This gives it a lower tolerance of noise than most other gift cultures, and goes a long way to explain both the taboo against posturing and the taboo against attacks on competence. Any significant incidence of flames over hackers' competence would intolerably disrupt the culture's reputation scoreboard.

The same vulnerability to noise explains the model of public humility required of the hacker community's tribal elders. They must be seen to be free of boast and posturing so the taboo against dangerous noise will hold [8].

Talking softly is also functional if one aspires to be a maintainer of a successful project; one must convince the community that one has good judgement, because most of the maintainer's job is going to be judging other people's code. Who would be inclined to contribute work to someone who clearly can't judge the quality of their own code, or whose behavior suggests they will attempt to unfairly hog the reputation return from the project? Potential contributors want project leaders with enough humility and class to be able to to say, when objectively appropriate, "Yes, that does work better than my version, I'll use it"—and to give credit where credit is due.

Yet another reason for humble behavior is that in the open source world, you seldom want to give the impression that a project is 'done'. This might lead a potential contributor not to feel needed. The way to maximize your leverage is to be humble about the state of the program. If one does one's bragging through the code, and then says, "Well shucks, it doesn't do x, y, and z, so it can't be that good", patches for x, y, and z will often swiftly follow.

Finally, I have personally observed that the self-deprecating behavior of some leading hackers reflects a real (and not unjustified) fear of becoming the object of a personality cult. Linus Torvalds and Larry Wall both provide clear and numerous examples of such avoidance behavior. Once, on a dinner expedition with Larry Wall, I joked, "You're the alpha hacker here—you get to pick the restaurant." He flinched noticeably. And rightly so; failing to distinguish their shared values from the personalities of their leaders has ruined a good many voluntary communities, a pattern of which Larry and Linus cannot fail to be fully aware. On the other hand, most hackers would love to have Larry's problem, if they could but bring themselves to admit it.

Global Implications of the Reputation-Game Model

The reputation-game analysis has some more implications that may not be immediately obvious. Many of these derive from the fact that one gains more prestige from founding a successful project than from cooperating in an existing one. One also gains more from projects that are strikingly innovative, as opposed to being 'me, too' incremental improvements on software that already exists. On the other hand, software that nobody but the author understands or has a need for is a non-starter in the reputation game, and it's often easier to attract good notice by contributing to an existing project than it is to get people to notice a new one. Finally, it's much harder to compete with an already successful project than it is to fill an empty niche.

Thus, there's an optimum distance from one's neighbors (the most similar competing projects). Too close and one's product will be a "me, too!" of limited value, a poor gift (one would be better off contributing to an existing project). Too far away, and nobody will be able to use, understand, or perceive the relevance of one's effort (again, a poor gift). This creates a pattern of homesteading in the noosphere that rather resembles that of settlers spreading into a physical frontier—not random, but like a diffusion-limited fractal. Projects tend to get started to fill functional gaps near the frontier (see endnote 9 for further discussion of the lure of novelty).

Some very successful projects become category killers; nobody wants to homestead anywhere near them because competing against the established base for the attention of hackers would be too hard. People who might otherwise found their own distinct efforts end up, instead, adding extensions for these big, successful projects. The classic category killer example is GNU Emacs; its variants fill the ecological niche for a fully-programmable editor so completely that no competitor has gotten much beyond the one-man project stage since the early 1980s. Instead, people write Emacs modes.

Globally, these two tendencies (gap-filling and category-killers) have driven a broadly predictable trend in project starts over time. In the 1970s most of the open source that existed was toys and demos. In the 1980s the push was in development and Internet tools. In the 1990s the action shifted to operating systems. In each case, a new and more difficult level of problems was attacked when the possibilities of the previous one had been nearly exhausted.

This trend has interesting implications for the near future. In early 1998, Linux looked very much like a category killer for the 'open-source operating systems' niche—people who might otherwise write competing operating systems are now writing Linux device drivers and extensions instead. And most of the lower-level tools the culture ever imagined having as open-source already exist. What's left?

Applications. As the third millenium begins, it seems safe to predict that open-source development effort will increasingly shift towards the last virgin territory—programs for non-techies. A clear early indicator was the development of GIMP (*http://www.gimp.org*), the Photoshop-like image workshop that is open source's first major application with the kind of end-user–friendly GUI interface considered *de rigueur* in commercial applications for the last decade. Another is the amount of buzz surrounding application-toolkit projects such as KDE (see *http://www.kde.org*) and GNOME (see *http://www.gnome.org*).

A respondent to this essay has pointed out that the homesteading analogy also explains why hackers react with such visceral anger to Microsoft's "embrace and extend" policy of complexifying and then closing up Internet protocols. The hacker culture can coexist with most closed software; the existence of Adobe Photoshop, for example, does not make the territory near GIMP (its open-source equivalent) significantly less attractive. But when Microsoft succeeds at de-commoditizing a protocol so that only Microsoft's own programmers can write software for it, they do not merely harm customers by extending their monopoly; they also reduce the amount and quality of noosphere available for hackers to homestead and cultivate[9]. No wonder hackers often refer to Microsoft's strategy as "protocol pollution"; they are reacting exactly like farmers watching someone poison the river they water their crops with!

Finally, the reputation-game analysis explains the oft-cited dictum that you do not become a hacker by calling yourself a hacker— you become a hacker when *other hackers* call you a hacker [10]. A hacker, considered in this light, is somebody who has shown (by contributing gifts) that he or she both has technical ability and understands how the reputation game works. This judgement is mostly one of awareness and acculturation, and can be delivered only by those already well inside the culture.

How Fine a Gift?

There are consistent patterns in the way the hacker culture values contributions and returns peer esteem for them. It's not hard to observe the following rules:

> 1. If it doesn't work as well as I have been led to expect it will, it's no good — no matter how clever and original it is.

Note the phrase "led to expect". This rule is not a demand for perfection; beta and experimental software is allowed to have bugs. It's a demand that the user be able to accurately estimate risks from the stage of the project and the developers' representations about it.

This rule underlies the fact that open-source software tends to stay in beta for a long time, and not get even a 1.0 version number until the developers are very sure it will not hand out a lot of nasty surprises. In the closed-source world, Version 1.0 means: "Don't touch this if you're prudent." In the open-source world, it reads something more like: "The developers are willing to bet their reputations on this."

2. WORK THAT EXTENDS THE NOOSPHERE IS BETTER THAN WORK THAT DUPLICATES AN EXISTING PIECE OF FUNC-TIONAL TERRITORY.

The naive way to put this would have been: *original work is better than mere duplication of the functions of existing software.* But it's not actually quite that simple. Duplicating the functions of existing *closed* software counts as highly as original work if by doing so you break open a closed protocol or format and make that territory newly available.

Thus, for example, one of the highest-prestige projects in the present open-source world is Samba—the code that allows Unix machines to act as clients or servers for Microsoft's proprietary SMB file-sharing protocol. There is very little creative work to be done here; it's mostly an issue of getting the reverse-engineered details right. Nevertheless, the members of the Samba group are perceived as heroes because they neutralize a Microsoft effort to lock in whole user populations and cordon off a big section of the noosphere.

3. WORK THAT MAKES IT INTO A MAJOR DISTRIBUTION IS BETTER THAN WORK THAT DOESN'T. WORK CARRIED IN ALL MAJOR DISTRIBUTIONS IS MOST PRESTIGIOUS.

The major distributions include not just the big Linux distributions like Red Hat, Debian, Caldera, and SuSE, but other collections that are understood to have reputations of their own to maintain and thus implicitly certify quality—like BSD distributions or the Free Software Foundation source collection.

4. UTILIZATION IS THE SINCEREST FORM OF FLATTERY — AND CATEGORY KILLERS ARE BETTER THAN ALSO-RANS.

Trusting the judgment of others is basic to the peer-review process. It's necessary because nobody has time to review all possible alternatives. So work used by lots of people is considered better than work used by a few.

To have done work so good that nobody cares to use the alternatives anymore is therefore to have earned huge prestige. The most possible peer esteem comes from having done widely popular, category-killing original work that is carried by all major distributions. People who have pulled this off more than once are half-seriously referred to as demigods.

> 5. CONTINUED DEVOTION TO HARD, BORING WORK (LIKE DEBUGGING, OR WRITING DOCUMENTATION) IS MORE PRAISEWORTHY THAN CHERRYPICKING THE FUN AND EASY HACKS.

This norm is how the community rewards necessary tasks that hackers would not naturally incline towards. It is to some extent contradicted by:

> 6. NONTRIVIAL EXTENSIONS OF FUNCTION ARE BETTER THAN LOW-LEVEL PATCHES AND DEBUGGING.

The way this seems to work is that on a one-shot basis, adding a feature is likely to get more reward than fixing a bug—unless the bug is exceptionally nasty or obscure, such that nailing it is itself a demonstration of unusual skill and cleverness. But when these behaviors are extended over time, a person with a long history of paying attention to and nailing even ordinary bugs may well outrank someone who has spent a similar amount of effort adding easy features.

A respondent has pointed out that these rules interact in interesting ways and do not necessarily reward highest possible utility all the time. Ask a hacker whether he's likely to become better known for a brand new tool of his own or for extensions to someone else's and the answer "new tool" will not be in doubt. But ask about (a) a brand new tool that is only used a few times a day invisibly by the OS but that rapidly becomes a category killer, versus (b) several extensions to an existing tool that are neither especially novel nor category-killers, but are daily used and daily visible to a huge number of users and you are likely to get some hesitation before the hacker settles on (a). These alternatives are about evenly stacked.

Said respondent gave this question point for me by adding: "Case (a) is fetchmail; case (b) is your many Emacs extensions, like *vc.el* and *gud.el*." And indeed he is correct; I am more likely to be tagged "the author of fetchmail" than "the author of a boatload of Emacs modes", even though the latter probably have had higher total utility over time.

What may be going on here is simply that work with a novel 'brand identity' gets more notice than work aggregated to an existing 'brand'. Elucidation of these rules, and what they tell us about the hacker culture's scoreboarding system, would make a good topic for further investigation.

NOOSPHERIC PROPERTY AND THE ETHOLOGY OF TERRITORY

To understand the causes and consequences of Lockean property customs, it will help us to look at them from yet another angle; that of animal ethology, specifically the ethology of territory.

Property is an abstraction of animal territoriality, which evolved as a way of reducing intraspecies violence. By marking his bounds, and respecting the bounds of others, a wolf diminishes his chances of being in a fight that could weaken or kill him and make him less reproductively successful. Similarly, the function of property in human societies is to prevent inter-human conflict by setting bounds that clearly separate peaceful behavior from aggression.

It is fashionable in some circles to describe human property as an arbitrary social convention, but this is dead wrong. Anybody who has ever owned a dog who barked when strangers came near its owner's property has experienced the essential continuity between animal territoriality and human property. Our domesticated cousins of the wolf know, instinctively, that property is no mere social convention or game, but a critically important evolved mechanism for the avoidance of violence. (This makes them smarter than a good many human political theorists.)

Claiming property (like marking territory) is a performative act, a way of declaring what boundaries will be defended. Community support of property claims is a way to minimize friction and maximize cooperative behavior. These things remain true even when the 'property claim' is much more abstract than a fence or a dog's bark, even when it's just the statement of the project maintainer's name in a README file. It's still an abstraction of territoriality, and (like other forms of property) based in territorial instincts evolved to assist conflict resolution.

This ethological analysis may at first seem very abstract and difficult to relate to actual hacker behavior. But it has some important consequences. One is in explaining the popularity of World Wide Web sites, and especially why open-source projects with websites seem so much more 'real' and substantial than those without them.

Considered objectively, this seems hard to explain. Compared to the effort involved in originating and maintaining even a small program, a web page is easy, so it's hard to consider a web page evidence of substance or unusual effort.

Nor are the functional characteristics of the Web itself sufficient explanation. The communication functions of a web page can be as well or better served by a combination of an FTP site, a mailing list, and Usenet postings. In fact it's quite unusual for a project's routine communications to be done over the Web rather than via a mailing list or newsgroup. Why, then, the popularity of websites as project homes?

The metaphor implicit in the term 'home page' provides an important clue. While founding an open-source project is a territorial claim in the noosphere (and customarily recognized as such) it is not a terribly compelling one on the psychological level. Software, after all, has no natural location and is instantly reduplicable. It's assimilable to our instinctive notions of 'territory' and 'property', but only after some effort.

A project home page concretizes an abstract homesteading in the space of possible programs by expressing it as 'home' territory in the more spatially-organized realm of the World Wide Web. Descending from the noosphere to 'cyberspace' doesn't get us all the way to the real world of fences and barking dogs yet, but it does hook the abstract property claim more securely to our instinctive wiring about territory. And this is why projects with web pages seem more 'real'.

This point is much strengthened by hyperlinks and the existence of good search engines. A project with a web page is much more likely to be noticed by somebody exploring its neighborhood in the noosphere; others will link to it, searches will find it. A web page is therefore a better advertisement, a more effective performative act, a stronger claim on territory.

This ethological analysis also encourages us to look more closely at mechanisms for handling conflict in the open-source culture. It leads us to expect that, in addition to maximizing reputation incentives, ownership customs should also have a role in preventing and resolving conflicts.

CAUSES OF CONFLICT

In conflicts over open-source software we can identify four major issues:

- Who gets to make binding decisions about a project?
- Who gets credit or blame for what?

- How to reduce duplication of effort and prevent rogue versions from complicating bug tracking?

- What is the Right Thing, technically speaking?

If we take a second look at the "What is the Right Thing" issue, however, it tends to vanish. For any such question, either there is an objective way to decide it accepted by all parties or there isn't. If there is, game over and everybody wins. If there isn't, it reduces to "Who decides?"

Accordingly, the three problems a conflict-resolution theory has to resolve about a project are (a) where the buck stops on design decisions, (b) how to decide which contributors are credited and how, and (c) how to keep a project group and product from fissioning into multiple branches.

The role of ownership customs in resolving issues (a) and (c) is clear. Custom affirms that the owners of the project make the binding decisions. We have previously observed that custom also exerts heavy pressure against dilution of ownership by forking.

It's instructive to notice that these customs make sense even if one forgets the reputation game and examines them from within a pure 'craftmanship' model of the hacker culture. In this view these customs have less to do with the dilution of reputation incentives than with protecting a craftsman's right to execute his vision in his chosen way.

The craftsmanship model is not, however, sufficient to explain hacker customs about issue (b), who gets credit for what—because a pure craftsman, one unconcerned with the reputation game, would have no motive to care. To analyze these, we need to take the Lockean theory one step further and examine conflicts and the operation of property rights *within* projects as well as *between* them.

PROJECT STRUCTURES AND OWNERSHIP

The trivial case is that in which the project has a single owner/ maintainer. In that case there is no possible conflict. The owner makes all decisions and collects all credit and blame. The only possible conflicts are over succession issues—who gets to be the new owner if the old one disappears or loses interest. The community also has an interest, under issue (c), in preventing forking. These interests are expressed by a cultural norm that an owner/ maintainer should publicly hand title to someone if he or she can no longer maintain the project.

The simplest non-trivial case is when a project has multiple co-maintainers working under a single 'benevolent dictator' who owns the project. Custom favors this mode for group projects; it has been shown to work on projects as large as the Linux kernel or Emacs, and solves the "who decides" problem in a way that is not obviously worse than any of the alternatives.

Typically, a benevolent-dictator organization evolves from an owner-maintainer organization as the founder attracts contributors. Even if the owner stays dictator, it introduces a new level of possible disputes over who gets credited for what parts of the project.

In this situation, custom places an obligation on the owner/dictator to credit contributors fairly (through, for example, appropriate mentions in README or history files). In terms of the Lockean property model, this means that by contributing to a project you earn part of its reputation return (positive or negative).

Pursuing this logic, we see that a benevolent dictator does not in fact own his entire project absolutely. Though he has the right to make binding decisions, he in effect trades away shares of the total reputation return in exchange for others' work. The analogy with sharecropping on a farm is almost irresistible, except that a contributor's name stays in the credits and continues to 'earn' to some degree even after that contributor is no longer active.

As benevolent-dictator projects add more participants, they tend to develop two tiers of contributors; ordinary contributors and co-developers. A typical path to becoming a co-developer is taking responsibility for a major subsystem of the project. Another is to take the role of 'lord high fixer', characterizing and fixing many bugs. In this way or others, co-developers are the contributors who make a substantial and continuing investment of time in the project.

The subsystem-owner role is particularly important for our analysis and deserves further examination. Hackers like to say that "authority follows responsibility". A co-developer who accepts maintainance responsibility for a given subsystem generally gets to control both the implementation of that subsystem and its interfaces with the rest of the project, subject only to correction by the project leader (acting as architect). We observe that this rule effectively creates enclosed properties on the Lockean model within a project, and has exactly the same conflict-prevention role as other property boundaries.

By custom, the 'dictator' or project leader in a project with co-developers is expected to consult with those co-developers on key decisions. This is especially so if the decision concerns a subsystem that a co-developer 'owns' (that is, has invested time in and taken responsibility for). A wise leader, recognizing the function of the project's internal property boundaries, will not lightly interfere with or reverse decisions made by subsystem owners.

Some very large projects discard the benevolent dictator model entirely. One way to do this is turn the co-developers into a voting committee (as with Apache). Another is rotating dictatorship, in which control is occasionally passed from one member to another within a circle of senior co-developers; the Perl developers organize themselves this way.

Such complicated arrangements are widely considered unstable and difficult. Clearly this perceived difficulty is largely a function of the known hazards of design-by-committee, and of committees themselves; these are problems the hacker culture consciously understands. However, I think some of the visceral discomfort hackers feel about committee or rotating-chair organizations is that they're hard to fit into the unconscious Lockean model hackers use for reasoning about the simpler cases. It's problematic, in these complex organizations, to do an accounting of either ownership in the sense of control or ownership of reputation returns. It's hard to see where the internal boundaries are, and thus hard to avoid conflict unless the group enjoys an exceptionally high level of harmony and trust.

CONFLICT AND CONFLICT RESOLUTION

We've seen that within projects, an increasing complexity of roles is expressed by a distribution of design authority and partial property rights. While this is an efficient way to distribute incentives, it also dilutes the authority of the project leader—most importantly, it dilutes the leader's authority to squash potential conflicts.

While technical arguments over design might seem the most obvious risk for internecine conflict, they are seldom a serious cause of strife. These are usually relatively easily resolved by the territorial rule that authority follows responsibility.

Another way of resolving conflicts is by seniority—if two contributors or groups of contributors have a dispute, and the dispute cannot be resolved objectively, and neither owns the territory of the dispute, the side that has put the most work into the project as a whole (that is, the side with the most property rights in the whole project) wins.

(Equivalently, the side with the least invested loses. Interestingly this happens to be the same heuristic that many relational database engines use to resolve deadlocks. When two threads are deadlocked over resources, the side with the least invested in the current transaction is selected as the deadlock victim and is terminated. This usually selects the longest running transaction, or the more senior, as the victor.)

These rules generally suffice to resolve most project disputes. When they do not, fiat of the project leader usually suffices. Disputes that survive both these filters are rare.

Conflicts do not, as a rule, become serious unless these two criteria ("authority follows responsibility" and "seniority wins") point in different directions, *and* the authority of the project leader is weak or absent. The most obvious case in which this may occur is a succession dispute following the disappearance of the project lead. I have been in one fight of this kind. It was ugly, painful, protracted, only resolved when all parties became exhausted enough to hand control to an outside person, and I devoutly hope I am never anywhere near anything of the kind again.

Ultimately, all of these conflict-resolution mechanisms rest on the entire hacker community's willingness to enforce them. The only available enforcement mechanisms are flaming and shunning—public condemnation of those who break custom, and refusal to cooperate with them after they have done so.

ACCULTURATION MECHANISMS AND THE LINK TO ACADEMIA

An early version of this essay posed the following research question: how does the community inform and instruct its members as to its customs? Are the customs self-evident or self-organizing at a semi-conscious level? Are they taught by example? Are they taught by explicit instruction?

Teaching by explicit instruction is clearly rare, if only because few explicit descriptions of the culture's norms have existed for instructional use up to now.

Many norms are taught by example. To cite one very simple case, there is a norm that every software distribution should have a file called README or READ.ME that contains first-look instructions for browsing the distribution. This convention has been well established since at least the early 1980s; it has even, occasionally, been written down. But one normally derives it from looking at many distributions.

On the other hand, some hacker customs are self-organizing once one has acquired a basic (perhaps unconscious) understanding of the reputation game. Most hackers never have to be taught the three taboos I listed earlier in this essay, or at least would claim if asked that they are self-evident rather than transmitted. This phenomenon invites closer analysis—and perhaps we can find its explanation in the process by which hackers acquire knowledge about the culture.

Many cultures use hidden clues (more precisely 'mysteries' in the religio/mystical sense) as an acculturation mechanism. These are secrets that are not revealed to outsiders, but are expected to be discovered or deduced by the aspiring newbie. To be accepted inside, one must demonstrate that one both understands the mystery and has learned it in a culturally sanctioned way.

The hacker culture makes unusually conscious and extensive use of such clues or tests. We can see this process operating at at least three levels:

- Password-like specific mysteries. As one example, there is a Usenet newsgroup called *alt.sysadmin.recovery* that has a very explicit such secret; you cannot post without knowing it, and knowing it is considered evidence you are fit to post. The regulars have a strong taboo against revealing this secret.

- The requirement of initiation into certain technical mysteries. One must absorb a good deal of technical knowledge before one can give valued gifts (e.g., one must know at least one of the major computer languages). This requirement functions in the large in the way hidden clues do in the small, as a filter for qualities (such as capability for abstract thinking, persistence, and mental flexibility) that are necessary to function in the culture.

- Social-context mysteries. One becomes involved in the culture through attaching oneself to specific projects. Each project is a live social context of hackers that the would-be contributor has to investigate and understand socially as well as technically in order to function. (Concretely, a common way one does this is by reading the project's web pages and/or email archives.) It is through these project groups that newbies experience the behavioral example of experienced hackers.

In the process of acquiring these mysteries, the would-be hacker picks up contextual knowledge that (after a while) does make the three taboos and other customs seem self-evident.

One might, incidentally, argue that the structure of the hacker gift culture itself is its own central mystery. One is not considered acculturated (concretely: no one will call you a hacker) until one demonstrates a gut-level understanding of the reputation game and its implied customs, taboos, and usages. But this is trivial; all cultures demand such understanding from would-be joiners. Furthermore the hacker culture evinces no desire to have its internal logic and folkways kept secret—or, at least, nobody has ever flamed me for revealing them!

Respondents to this essay too numerous to list have pointed out that hacker ownership customs seem intimately related to (and may derive directly from) the practices of the academic world, especially the scientific research commmunity. This research community has similar problems in mining a territory of potentially productive ideas, and exhibits very similar adaptive solutions to those problems in the ways it uses peer review and reputation.

Since many hackers have had formative exposure to academia (it's common to learn how to hack while in college), the extent to which academia shares adaptive patterns with the hacker culture is of more than casual interest in understanding how these customs are applied.

Obvious parallels with the hacker 'gift culture', as I have characterized it, abound in academia. Once a researcher achieves tenure, there is no need to worry about survival issues. (Indeed, the concept of tenure can probably be traced back to an earlier gift culture in which "natural philosophers" were primarily wealthy gentlemen with time on their hands to devote to research.) In the absence of survival issues, reputation enhancement becomes the driving goal, which encourages sharing of new ideas and research through journals and other media. This makes objective functional sense because scientific research, like the hacker culture, relies heavily on the idea of 'standing upon the shoulders of giants', and not having to rediscover basic principles over and over again.

Some have gone so far as to suggest that hacker customs are merely a reflection of the research community's folkways and have actually (in most cases) been acquired there by individual hackers. This probably overstates the case, if only because hacker custom seems to be readily acquired by intelligent high-schoolers!

GIFT OUTCOMPETES EXCHANGE

There is a more interesting possibility here. I suspect academia and the hacker culture share adaptive patterns not because they're genetically related, but because they've both evolved the one most optimal social organization for what they're trying to do, given the laws of nature and the instinctive wiring of human beings. The verdict of history seems to be that free-market capitalism is the globally optimal way to cooperate for economic efficiency; perhaps, in a similar way, the reputation-game gift culture is the globally optimal way to cooperate for generating (and checking!) high-quality creative work.

Support for this theory comes from a large body of psychological studies on the interaction between art and reward [11]. These studies have received less attention than they should, in part perhaps because their popularizers have shown a tendency to overinterpret them into general attacks against the free market and intellectual

THE CATHEDRAL AND THE BAZAAR

property. Nevertheless, their results do suggest that some kinds of scarcity-economics rewards actually decrease the productivity of creative workers such as programmers.

Psychologist Theresa Amabile of Brandeis University, cautiously summarizing the results of a 1984 study of motivation and reward, observed: "It may be that commissioned work will, in general, be less creative than work that is done out of pure interest." Amabile goes on to observe: "The more complex the activity, the more it's hurt by extrinsic reward." Interestingly, the studies suggest that flat salaries don't demotivate, but piecework rates and bonuses do.

Thus, it may be economically smart to give performance bonuses to people who flip burgers or dig ditches, but it's probably smarter to decouple salary from performance in a programming shop and let people choose their own projects (both trends that the open-source world takes to their logical conclusions). Indeed, these results suggest that the only time it is a good idea to reward performance in programming is when the programmer is so motivated that he or she would have worked without the reward!

Other researchers in the field are willing to point a finger straight at the issues of autonomy and creative control that so preoccupy hackers. "To the extent one's experience of being self-determined is limited," said Richard Ryan, associate psychology professor at the University of Rochester, "one's creativity will be reduced as well."

In general, presenting any task as a means rather than an end in itself seems to demotivate. Even winning a competition with others or gaining peer esteem can be demotivating in this way if the victory is experienced as work for reward (which may explain why hackers are culturally prohibited from explicitly seeking or claiming that esteem).

To complicate the management problem further, controlling verbal feedback seems to be just as demotivating as piecework payment.

Ryan found that corporate employees who were told, "Good, you're doing as you *should*" were "significantly less intrinsically motivated than those who received feedback informationally."

It may still be intelligent to offer incentives, but they have to come without attachments to avoid gumming up the works. There is a critical difference (Ryan observes) between saying, "I'm giving you this reward because I recognize the value of your work," and "You're getting this reward because you've lived up to my standards." The first does not demotivate; the second does.

In these psychological observations we can ground a case that an open-source development group will be substantially more productive (especially over the long term, in which creativity becomes more critical as a productivity multiplier) than an equivalently sized and skilled group of closed-source programmers (de)motivated by scarcity rewards.

This suggests from a slightly different angle one of the speculations in *The Cathedral and the Bazaar*; that, ultimately, the industrial/factory mode of software production was doomed to be outcompeted from the moment capitalism began to create enough of a wealth surplus that many programmers could live in a post-scarcity gift culture.

Indeed, it seems the prescription for highest software productivity is almost a Zen paradox; if you want the most efficient production, you must give up trying to *make* programmers produce. Handle their subsistence, give them their heads, and forget about deadlines. To a conventional manager this sounds crazily indulgent and doomed—but it is *exactly* the recipe with which the open-source culture is now clobbering its competition.

CONCLUSION: FROM CUSTOM TO CUSTOMARY LAW

We have examined the customs that regulate the ownership and control of open-source software. We have seen how they imply an underlying theory of property rights homologous to the Lockean theory of land tenure. We have related that to an analysis of the hacker culture as a gift culture in which participants compete for prestige by giving time, energy, and creativity away. We have examined the implications of this analysis for conflict resolution in the culture.

The next logical question to ask is: "Why does this matter?" Hackers developed these customs without conscious analysis and (up to now) have followed them without conscious analysis. It's not immediately clear that conscious analysis has gained us anything practical—unless, perhaps, we can move from description to prescription and deduce ways to improve the functioning of these customs.

We have found a close logical analogy for hacker customs in the theory of land tenure under the Anglo-American common-law tradition. Historically [12], the European tribal cultures that invented this tradition improved their dispute-resolution systems by moving from a system of unarticulated, semi-conscious custom to a body of explicit customary law memorized by tribal wisemen—and eventually, written down.

Perhaps, as our population rises and acculturation of all new members becomes more difficult, it is time for the hacker culture to do something analogous—to develop written codes of good practice for resolving the various sorts of disputes that can arise in connection with open-source projects, and a tradition of arbitration in which senior members of the community may be asked to mediate disputes.

The analysis in this essay suggests the outlines of what such a code might look like, making explicit that which was previously implicit. No such codes could be imposed from above; they would have to be voluntarily adopted by the founders or owners of individual projects. Nor could they be completely rigid, as the pressures on the culture are likely to change over time. Finally, for enforcement of such codes to work, they would have to reflect a broad consensus of the hacker tribe.

I have begun work on such a code, tentatively titled the "Malvern Protocol" after the little town where I live. If the general analysis in this paper becomes sufficiently widely accepted, I will make the Malvern Protocol publicly available as a model code for dispute resolution. Parties interested in critiquing and developing this code, or just offering feedback on whether they think it's a good idea or not, are invited to contact me by email, *esr@thyrsus.com*.

Questions for Further Research

The culture's (and my own) understanding of large projects that don't follow a benevolent-dictator model is weak. Most such projects fail. A few become spectacularly successful and important (Perl, Apache, KDE). Nobody really understands where the difference lies. There's a vague sense abroad that each such project is *sui generis* and stands or falls on the group dynamic of its particular members, but is this true or are there replicable strategies that a group can follow?

THE MAGIC CAULDRON

✦ ✦ ✦

This essay analyzes the evolving economic substrate of the open-source phenomenon. I first explode some prevalent myths about the funding of program development and the price structure of software. I then present a game-theory analysis of the stability of open-source cooperation. I present nine models for sustainable funding of open-source development; two non-profit, seven for-profit. I then continue to develop a qualitative theory of when it is economically rational for software to be closed. I then examine some novel additional mechanisms the market is now inventing to fund for-profit open-source development, including the reinvention of the patronage system and task markets. I conclude with some tentative predictions of the future.

INDISTINGUISHABLE FROM MAGIC

In Welsh myth, the goddess Ceridwen owned a great cauldron that would magically produce nourishing food—when commanded by a spell known only to the goddess. In modern science, Buckminster Fuller gave us the concept of 'ephemeralization', technology becoming both more effective and less expensive as the physical resources invested in early designs are replaced by more and more information content. Arthur C. Clarke connected the two by observing that "Any sufficiently advanced technology is indistinguishable from magic".

To many people, the successes of the open-source community seem like an implausible form of magic. High-quality software materializes for free, which is nice while it lasts but hardly seems sustainable in the real world of competition and scarce resources. What's the catch? Is Ceridwen's cauldron just a conjuring trick? And if not, how does ephemeralization work in this context—what spell is the goddess speaking?

BEYOND GEEKS BEARING GIFTS

The experience of the open-source culture has certainly confounded many of the assumptions of people who learned about software development outside it. *The Cathedral and the Bazaar* described the ways in which decentralized cooperative software development effectively overturns Brooks's Law, leading to unprecedented levels of reliability and quality on individual projects. *Homesteading the Noosphere*, examined the social dynamics within which this 'bazaar' style of development is situated, arguing that it is most effectively understood not in conventional exchange-economy terms but as what anthropologists call a gift culture in which members compete for status by giving things away. In this essay I begin by exploding some common myths about software production economics; then continue the line of analysis of these essays into the realm of economics, game theory and business models, developing new conceptual tools needed to understand the way that the gift culture of open-source developers can sustain itself in an exchange economy.

In order to pursue this line of analysis without distraction, we'll need to abandon (or at least agree to temporarily ignore) the gift-culture level of explanation. *Homesteading the Noosphere* posited that gift culture behavior arises in situations where survival goods are abundant enough to make the exchange game no longer very interesting; but while this appears sufficiently powerful as a *psychological* explanation of behavior, it lacks suffiency as an explanation of the mixed *economic* context in which most open-source developers actually operate. For most, the exchange game has lost its appeal but not its power to constrain. Their behavior has to make sufficient material-scarcity–economics sense to keep them in a gift-culture–supporting zone of surplus.

Therefore, this essay will consider (from entirely *within* the realm of scarcity economics) the modes of cooperation and exchange that sustain open-source development. While doing so it will answer the pragmatic question "How do I make money at this?" in detail and with examples. First, though, I will show that much of the tension behind that question derives from prevailing folk models of software-production economics that are false to fact.

(A final note before the exposition: the discussion and advocacy of open-source development in this essay should not be construed as a case that closed-source development is intrinsically wrong, nor as a brief against intellectual-property rights in software, nor as an altruistic appeal to 'share'. While these arguments are still beloved to a vocal minority in the open-source development community, experience since *The Cathedral and the Bazaar* was published has made it clear that they are unnecessary. An entirely sufficient case for open-source development rests on its engineering and economic outcomes—better quality, higher reliability, lower costs, and increased choice.)

THE MANUFACTURING DELUSION

We need to begin by noticing that computer programs, like all other kinds of tools or capital goods, have two distinct kinds of economic value. They have *use value* and *sale value*.

The use value of a program is its economic value as a tool, a productivity multiplier. The sale value of a program is its value as a salable commodity. (In professional economist-speak, sale value is value as a final good, and use value is value as an intermediate good.)

When most people try to reason about software-production economics, they tend to assume a 'factory model', which is founded on the following fundamental premises:

- Most developer time is paid for by sale value.

- The sale value of software is proportional to its development cost (i.e., the cost of the resources required to functionally replicate it) and to its use value.

In other words, people have a strong tendency to assume that software has the value characteristics of a typical manufactured good. But both of these assumptions are demonstrably false.

First, code written for sale is only the tip of the programming iceberg. In the pre-microcomputer era it used to be a commonplace that 90% of all the code in the world was written in-house at banks and insurance companies. This is probably no longer the case—other industries are much more software-intensive now, and the finance industry's share of the total must have accordingly dropped—but we'll see shortly that there is empirical evidence that approximately 95% of code is still written in-house.

This code includes most of the stuff of MIS, the financial- and database-software customizations every medium and large company needs. It includes technical-specialist code like device drivers. Almost nobody makes money selling device drivers, a point we'll return to later. It includes all kinds of embedded code for our increasingly microchip-driven machines—from machine tools and jet airliners to cars to microwave ovens and toasters.

Most such in-house code is integrated with its environment in ways that make reusing or copying it very difficult. (This is true whether the environment is a business office's set of procedures or the fuel-injection system of a combine harvester.) Thus, as the environment changes, work is continually needed to keep the software in step.

This is called maintenance, and any software engineer or systems analyst will tell you that it makes up the vast majority (more than 75%) of what programmers get paid to do. Accordingly, most programmer-hours are spent (and most programmer salaries are paid for) writing or maintaining in-house code that has no sale value at all—a fact the reader may readily check by examining the listings of programming jobs in any newspaper with a 'Help Wanted' section.

Scanning the employment section of your local newspaper is an enlightening experiment that I urge the reader to perform for him- or herself. Examine the jobs listings under programming, data processing, and software engineering for positions that involve the development of software. Categorize each such job according to whether the software is being developed for use or for sale.

It will quickly become clear that, even given the most inclusive definition of "for sale", at least 19 in 20 of the salaries offered are being funded strictly by use value (that is, value as an intermediate good). This is our reason for believing that only 5% of the industry is sale-value–driven. Note, however, that the rest of the analysis in this essay is relatively insensitive to this number; if it were 15% or even 20%, the economic consequences would remain essentially the same.

When I speak at technical conferences, I usually begin my talk by asking two questions: how many in the audience are paid to write software, and for how many do their salaries depend on the sale value of software. I generally get a forest of hands for the first question, few or none for the second, and considerable audience surprise at the proportion.

Second, the theory that the sale value of software is coupled to its development or replacement costs is even more easily demolished by examining the actual behavior of consumers. There are many goods for which a proportion of this kind actually holds (before depreciation)—food, cars, machine tools. There are even many intangible goods for which sale value couples strongly to development and replacement cost—rights to reproduce music or maps or databases, for example. Such goods may retain or even increase their sale value after their original vendor is gone.

By contrast, when a software product's vendor goes out of business (or if the product is merely discontinued), the maximum price consumers will pay for it rapidly falls to near zero regardless of its theoretical use value or the development cost of a functional equivalent. (To check this assertion, examine the remainder bins at any software store near you.)

The behavior of retailers when a vendor folds is very revealing. It tells us that they know something the vendors don't. What they know is this: the price a consumer will pay is effectively capped by the *expected future value of vendor service* (where "service" is here construed broadly to include enhancements, upgrades, and follow-on projects).

In other words, software is largely a service industry operating under the persistent but unfounded delusion that it is a manufacturing industry.

It is worth examining why we normally tend to believe otherwise. It may simply be because the small portion of the software industry that manufactures for sale is also the only part that advertises its product. The common mental bias that regards manufacturing as more 'real' than services, because it produces things you can heft, may be at work [1]. Also, some of the most visible and heavily advertised products are ephemera like games that have little in the way of continuing service requirements (the exception, rather than the rule) [2].

It is also worth noting that the manufacturing delusion encourages price structures that are pathologically out of line with the actual breakdown of development costs. If (as is generally accepted) over 75% of a typical software project's life-cycle costs will be in maintenance and debugging and extensions, then the common price policy of charging a high fixed purchase price and relatively low or zero support fees is bound to lead to results that serve all parties poorly.

Consumers lose because, even though software is a service industry, the incentives in the factory model all work against a vendor's offering *competent* service. If the vendor's money comes from selling bits, most effort will go into making bits and shoving them out the door; the help desk, not a profit center, will become a dumping ground for the least effective employees and get only enough resources to avoid actively alienating a critical number of customers.

It gets worse. Actual use means service calls, which cut into the profit margin unless you're charging for service. In the open-source world, you seek the largest possible user base, so as to get maximum feedback and the most vigorous possible secondary markets; in the closed-source you seek as many buyers but as few actual users as possible. Therefore the logic of the factory model most strongly rewards vendors who produce shelfware—software that is sufficiently well marketed to make sales but actually useless in practice.

The other side of this coin is that most vendors buying this factory model will also fail in the longer run. Funding indefinitely-continuing support expenses from a fixed price is only viable in a market that is expanding quickly enough to cover the support and life-cycle costs entailed in yesterday's sales with tomorrow's revenues. Once a market matures and sales slow down, most vendors will have no choice but to cut expenses by orphaning the product [3].

Whether this is done explicitly (by discontinuing the product) or implicitly (by making support hard to get), it has the effect of driving customers to competitors—because it destroys the product's expected future value, which is contingent on that service. In the short run, one can escape this trap by making bug-fix releases pose as new products with a new price attached, but consumers quickly tire of this. In the long run, therefore, the only way to escape is to have no competitors—that is, to have an effective monopoly on one's market. In the end, there can be only one.

And, indeed, we have repeatedly seen this support-starvation failure mode kill off even strong second-place competitors in a market niche. (The pattern should be particularly clear to anyone who has ever surveyed the history of proprietary PC operating systems, word processors, accounting programs, or business software in general.) The perverse incentives set up by the factory model lead to a winner-take-all market dynamic in which even the winner's customers end up losing.

If not the factory model, then what? To handle the real cost structure of the software life cycle efficiently (in both the informal and economics-jargon senses of "efficiency"), we require a price structure founded on service contracts, subscriptions, and a *continuing* exchange of value between vendor and customer. This is already the price structure of the largest merchant software products such as ERP (Enterprise Resource Planning) systems, for which the development costs are so large that no fixed purchase price could possibly cover them; firms like Baan and Peoplesoft actually make their money from after-sale consulting fees. Under the efficiency-seeking conditions of the free market we can predict that this is the sort of price structure most of a mature software industry will ultimately follow.

The foregoing begins to give us some insight into why open-source software increasingly poses not merely a technological but an economic challenge to the prevailing order. The effect of making software 'free', it seems, is to force us into that service-fee–dominated world—and to expose what a relatively weak prop the sale value of the secret bits in closed-source software was all along.

This transition will not be quite the wrench it may at first appear. Many consumers find that pirate copies of packaged software (especially games, operating systems, and popular productivity tools) are readily available to them. Thus, many proprietary software sale prices are, from the point of view of the consumer, only worth paying as claims on other goods: vendor support, or the paper manuals, or a feeling of virtuousness. Commercial distributions of so-called 'free' software often justify their price to the customer in exactly the same way—the only difference is that their vendors do not fool themselves into thinking that the bits alone necessarily have value to the customer.

The term 'free' is misleading in another way as well. Lowering the cost of a good tends to increase, rather than decrease, total investment in the people and infrastructure that sustains it. When the price of cars goes down, the demand for auto mechanics goes up—which is why even those 5% of programmers now compensated by sale-value would be very unlikely to suffer in an open-source world. The people who lose in the transition won't be programmers, they will be investors who have bet on closed-source strategies where they're not economically viable.

THE "INFORMATION WANTS TO BE FREE" MYTH

There is another myth, equal and opposite to the factory-model delusion, which often confuses people's thinking about the economics of open-source software. It is that "information wants to be free". This usually unpacks to a claim that the zero marginal cost of reproducing digital information implies that its clearing price ought to be zero (or that a market full of duplicators will force it to zero).

Some kinds of information really do want to be free, in the weak sense that their value goes up as more people have access to them—a technical standards document is a good example. But the myth that *all* information wants to be free is readily exploded by considering the value of information that constitutes a privileged pointer to a rivalrous good—a treasure map, say, or a Swiss bank account number, or a claim on services such as a computer account password. Even though the claiming information can be duplicated at zero cost, the item being claimed cannot be. Hence, the nonzero marginal cost for the item can be inherited by the claiming information.

We mention this myth mainly to assert that it is almost unrelated to the economic-utility arguments for open source; as we'll see later, those would generally hold up well even under the assumption that software actually *does* have the (nonzero) value structure of a manufactured good. We therefore have no need to tackle the question of whether software 'should' be free or not.

THE INVERSE COMMONS

Having cast a skeptical eye on one prevailing model, let's see if we can build another—a hard-nosed economic explanation of what makes open-source cooperation sustainable.

This is a question that bears examination on a couple of different levels. On one level, we need to explain the behavior of individuals who contribute to open-source projects; on another, we need to understand the economic forces that sustain cooperation on open-source projects like Linux or Apache.

Again, we must first demolish a widespread folk model that interferes with understanding. Over every attempt to explain cooperative behavior there looms the shadow of Garret Hardin's "Tragedy of the Commons".

Hardin famously asks us to imagine a green held in common by a village of peasants, who graze their cattle there. But grazing degrades the commons, tearing up grass and leaving muddy patches, which re-grow their cover only slowly. If there is no agreed-upon (and enforced!) policy to allocate grazing rights that prevents overgrazing, all parties' incentives push them to run as many cattle as quickly as possible, trying to extract maximum value before the commons degrades into a sea of mud.

Most people have an intuitive model of cooperative behavior that goes much like this. The tragedy of the commons actually stems from two linked problems, one of overuse and another of under-provision. On the demand side, the commons situation encourages a race to the bottom by overuse—what economists call a congested–public-good problem. On the supply side, the commons rewards free-rider behavior—removing or diminishing incentives for individual actors to invest in developing more pasturage.

The tragedy of the commons predicts only three possible outcomes. One is the sea of mud. Another is for some actor with coercive power to enforce an allocation policy on behalf of the village (the communist solution). The third is for the commons to break up as village members fence off bits they can defend and manage sustainably (the property-rights solution).

When people reflexively apply this model to open-source cooperation, they expect it to be unstable with a short half-life. Since there's no obvious way to enforce an allocation policy for programmer time over the Internet, this model leads straight to a prediction that the commons will break up, with various bits of software being taken closed-source and a rapidly decreasing amount of work being fed back into the communal pool.

In fact, it is empirically clear that the trend is opposite to this. The trend in breadth and volume of open-source development can be measured by submissions per day at Metalab and SourceForge (the leading Linux source sites) or announcements per day at freshmeat.net (a site dedicated to advertising new software releases). Volume on both is steadily and rapidly increasing. Clearly there is some critical way in which the "Tragedy of the Commons" model fails to capture what is actually going on.

Part of the answer certainly lies in the fact that using software does not decrease its value. Indeed, widespread use of open-source software tends to *increase* its value, as users fold in their own fixes and features (code patches). In this inverse commons, the grass grows taller when it's grazed upon.

That this public good cannot be degraded by overuse takes care of half of Hardin's tragedy, the congested–public-goods problem. It doesn't explain why open source doesn't suffer from underprovision. Why don't people who know the open-source community exists universally exhibit free-rider behavior, waiting for others to do the work they need, or (if they do the work themselves) not bothering to contribute the work back into the commons?

Part of the answer lies in the fact that people don't merely need solutions, they need solutions *on time*. It's seldom possible to predict when someone else will finish a given piece of needed work. If the payoff from fixing a bug or adding a feature is sufficient to any potential contributor, that person will dive in and do it (at which point the fact that everyone else is a free rider becomes irrelevant).

Another part of the answer lies in the fact that the putative market value of small patches to a common source base is hard to capture. Suppose I write a fix for an irritating bug, and suppose many people realize the fix has money value; how do I collect from all those people? Conventional payment systems have high enough overheads to make this a real problem for the sorts of micropayments that would usually be appropriate.

It may be more to the point that this value is not merely hard to capture, in the general case it's hard to even *assign*. As a thought experiment, let us suppose that the Internet came equipped with the theoretically ideal micropayment system—secure, universally accessible, zero-overhead. Now let's say you have written a patch labeled "Miscellaneous Fixes to the Linux Kernel". How do you know what price to ask? How would a potential buyer, not having seen the patch yet, know what is reasonable to pay for it?

What we have here is almost like a funhouse-mirror image of F. A. Hayek's 'calculation problem'—it would take a superbeing, both able to evaluate the functional worth of patches and trusted to set prices accordingly, to lubricate trade.

Unfortunately, there's a serious superbeing shortage, so patch author J. Random Hacker is left with two choices: sit on the patch, or throw it into the pool for free.

Sitting on the patch gains nothing. Indeed, it incurs a future cost—the effort involved in re-merging the patch into the source base in each new release. So the payoff from this choice is actually negative (and multiplied by the rapid release tempo characteristic of open-source projects).

To put it more positively, the contributor gains by passing maintainance overhead of the patch to the source-code owners and the rest of the project group. He also gains because others will improve on his work in the future. Finally, because he won't have to maintain the patch himself, he will be able to afford more time on other and larger customizations to suit his needs. The same arguments that favor opening source for entire packages apply to patches as well.

Throwing the patch in the pool may gain nothing, or it may encourage reciprocal effort from others that will address some of

J. Random's problems in the future. This choice, apparently altruistic, is actually optimally selfish in a game-theoretic sense.

In analyzing this kind of cooperation, it is important to note that while there is a free-rider problem (work may be underprovided in the absence of money or money-equivalent compensation) it is not one that scales with the number of end users (see endnote 1 for discussion). The complexity and communications overhead of an open-source project is almost entirely a function of the number of developers involved; having more end users who never look at source costs effectively nothing. It may increase the rate of silly questions appearing on the project mailing lists, but this is relatively easily forestalled by maintaining a Frequently Asked Questions list and blithely ignoring questioners who have obviously not read it (and in fact both these practices are typical).

The real free-rider problems in open-source software are more a function of friction costs in submitting patches than anything else. A potential contributor with little stake in the cultural reputation game (see *Homesteading the Noosphere*) may, in the absence of money compensation, think "It's not worth submitting this fix because I'll have to clean up the patch, write a ChangeLog entry, and sign the FSF assignment papers...." It's for this reason that the number of contributors (and, at second order, the success of) projects is strongly and inversely correlated with the number of hoops each project makes a contributing user go through. Such friction costs may be political as well as mechanical. Together I think they explain why the loose, amorphous Linux culture has attracted orders of magnitude more cooperative energy than the more tightly organized and centralized BSD efforts—and why the Free Software Foundation has receded in relative importance as Linux has risen.

This is all good as far as it goes. But it is an after-the-fact explanation of what J. Random Hacker does with his patch after he has created it. The other half we need is an economic explanation of how JRH was able to write that patch in the first place, rather than having to work on a closed-source program that might have returned him sale value. What business models create niches in which open-source development can flourish?

REASONS FOR CLOSING SOURCE

Before taxonomizing open-source business models, we should deal with exclusion payoffs in general. What exactly are we protecting when we close source?

Let's say you hire someone to write to order (say) a specialized accounting package for your business. That problem won't be solved any better if the sources are closed rather than open; the only rational reasons you might want them to be closed is if you want to sell the package to other people, or deny its use to competitors.

The obvious answer is that you're protecting sale value, but for the 95% of software written for internal use this doesn't apply. So what other gains are there in being closed?

That second case (protecting competitive advantage) bears a bit of examination. Suppose you open-source that accounting package. It becomes popular and benefits from improvements made by the community. Now your competitor starts to use it. The competitor gets the benefit without paying the development cost and cuts into your business. Is this an argument against open-sourcing?

Maybe—and maybe not. The real question is whether your gain from spreading the development load exceeds your loss due to increased competition from the free rider. Many people tend to reason poorly about this tradeoff through (a) ignoring the functional advantage of recruiting more development help, and (b) not treating the development costs as sunk. By hypothesis, you had to pay the development costs anyway, so counting them as a cost of open-sourcing (if you choose to do that) is mistaken.

Another reason often cited is the fear that disclosing source of a particular special accounting function might be tantamount to revealing confidential aspects of your business plan. This is really an argument not for closed source but against bad design; in a properly-written accounting package, business knowledge should not be expressed in code at all but rather in a schema or specification language implemented by the accounting engine (for a closely parallel case, consider the way that database schemas separate business knowledge from the mechanics of the database engine). The separation of function would enable you to guard the crown jewels (the schema) while getting maximum benefit from open-sourcing the engine.

There are other reasons for closing source that are outright irrational. You might, for example, be laboring under the delusion that closing the sources will make your business systems more secure against crackers and intruders. If so, I recommend therapeutic conversation with a cryptographer immediately. The really professional paranoids know better than to trust the security of closed-source programs, because they've learned through hard experience not to. Security is an aspect of reliability; only algorithms and implementations that have been thoroughly peer-reviewed can possibly be trusted as secure.

USE-VALUE FUNDING MODELS

A key fact that the distinction between use and sale value allows us to notice is that only *sale value* is threatened by the shift from closed to open source; use value is not.

If use value rather than sale value is really the major driver of software development, and (as was argued in *The Cathedral and the Bazaar*) open-source development is really more effective and efficient than closed, then we should expect to find circumstances in which expected use value alone sustainably funds open-source development.

And in fact it is not difficult to identify at least two important models in which full-time developer salaries for open-source projects are funded strictly out of use value.

THE APACHE CASE: COST-SHARING

Let's say you work for a firm that has a business-critical requirement for a high-volume, high-reliability web server. Maybe it's for electronic commerce, maybe you're a high-visibility media outlet selling advertising, maybe you're a portal site. You need 24/7 uptime, you need speed, and you need customizability.

How are you going to get these things? There are three basic strategies you can pursue:

Buy a proprietary web server.

In this case, you are betting that the vendor's agenda matches yours and that the vendor has the technical competence to implement properly. Even assuming both these things to be true, the product is likely to come up short in customizability; you will be able to modify it only through the hooks the vendor has chosen to provide. We can see from the monthly Netcraft surveys that this proprietary path is not a popular one and is getting less popular all the time.

Roll your own.

Building your own web server is not an option to dismiss instantly; web servers are not very complex, certainly less so than browsers, and a specialized one can be very lean and mean. Going this path, you can get the exact features and customizability you want, though you'll pay for it in development time. Your firm may also find it has a problem when you retire or leave.

Join the Apache group.

The Apache server was built by an Internet-connected group of webmasters who realized that it was smarter to pool their efforts into improving one code base than to run a large number of parallel development efforts. By doing this they were able to capture both most of the advantages of roll-your-own and the powerful debugging effect of massively-parallel peer review.

The advantage of the Apache choice is very strong. Just how strong, we may judge from the monthly Netcraft survey, which has shown Apache steadily gaining market share against all proprietary web servers since its inception. As of November 2000, Apache and its derivatives had 60% market share (*http://www.netcraft.com/survey/*)—with no legal owner, no promotion, and no contracted service organization behind it at all.

The Apache story generalizes to a model in which competing software users find it to their advantage to cooperatively fund open-source development because doing so gets them a better product, at lower cost, than they could otherwise have.

THE CISCO CASE: RISK-SPREADING

Some years ago, two programmers at Cisco (the networking-equipment manufacturer) got assigned the job of writing a distributed print-spooling system for use on Cisco's corporate network. This was quite a challenge. Besides supporting the ability for arbitrary user A to print at arbitrary printer B (which might be in the next room or a thousand miles away), the system had to make sure that in the event of a paper-out or toner-low condition the job would get rerouted to an alternate printer near the target. The system also needed to be able to report such problems to a printer administrator.

The duo came up with a clever set of modifications (*http://www.tpp.org/CiscoPrint/*) to the standard Unix print-spooler software, plus some wrapper scripts, that did the job. Then they realized that they, and Cisco, had a problem.

The problem was that neither of them was likely to be at Cisco forever. Eventually, both programmers would be gone, and the software would be unmaintained and begin to rot (that is, to gradually fall out of sync with real-world conditions). No developer likes to see this happen to his or her work, and the intrepid duo felt Cisco had paid for a solution under the not unreasonable expectation that it would outlast their own employment there.

Accordingly, they went to their manager and urged him to autho-
rize the release of the print-spooler software as open source. Their
argument was that Cisco would have no sale value to lose, and
much else to gain. By encouraging the growth of a community of
users and co-developers spread across many corporations, Cisco
could effectively hedge against the loss of the software's original
developers.

The Cisco story shows open source can function not only to lower
costs but to spread and mitigate risk. All parties find that the
openness of the source, and the presence of a collaborative community funded by multiple independent revenue streams, provides
a fail-safe that is itself economically valuable—sufficiently valuable to attract funding for it.

WHY SALE VALUE IS PROBLEMATIC

Open source makes it rather difficult to capture direct sale value
from software. The difficulty is not technical; source code is no
more nor less easily copied than binaries, and the enforcement of
copyright and license laws permitting capture of sale value would
not by necessity be any more difficult for open-source products
than it is for closed.

The difficulty lies rather with the nature of the social contract that
supports open-source development. For three mutually reinforcing
reasons, the major open-source licenses prohibit most of the sort
of restrictions on use, redistribution and modification that facili-
tate direct-sale revenue capture. To understand these reasons, we
must examine the social context within which the licenses evolved;
the Internet hacker culture (*http://www.tuxedo.org/˜esr/faqs/
hacker-howto.html*).

Despite myths about the hacker culture still too widely believed
outside it, none of these reasons has to do with hostility to the
market. While a minority of hackers does indeed remain hostile to
the profit motive, the general willingness of the community to
cooperate with for-profit Linux packagers like Red Hat, SuSE, and

Caldera demonstrates that most hackers will happily work with the corporate world when it serves their ends. The real reasons hackers frown on direct–revenue-capture licenses are more subtle and interesting.

One reason has to do with symmetry. While most open-source developers do not intrinsically object to others profiting from their gifts, most also demand that no party (with the possible exception of the originator of a piece of code) be in a *privileged* position to extract profits. J. Random Hacker is willing for Fubarco to profit by selling his software or patches, but only so long as JRH himself could also potentially do so.

Another has to do with unintended consequences. Hackers have observed that licenses that include restrictions on and fees for commercial use or sale (the most common form of attempt to recapture direct sale value, and not at first blush an unreasonable one) have serious chilling effects. A specific one is to cast a legal shadow on activities like redistribution in inexpensive CD-ROM anthologies, which we would ideally like to encourage. More generally, restrictions on use/sale/modification/distribution (and other complications in licensing) exact an overhead for conformance tracking and (as the number of packages people deal with rises) a combinatorial explosion of perceived uncertainty and potential legal risk. This outcome is considered harmful, and there is therefore strong social pressure to keep licenses simple and free of restrictions.

The final and most critical reason has to do with preserving the peer-review, gift-culture dynamic described in *Homesteading the Noosphere*. License restrictions designed to protect intellectual property or capture direct sale value often have the effect of making it legally impossible to fork the project. This is the case, for example, with Sun's so-called "Community Source" licenses for Jini and Java. While forking is frowned upon and considered a last resort (for reasons discussed at length in *Homesteading the Noosphere*), it's considered critically important that that last resort be present in case of maintainer incompetence or defection (e.g., to a more closed license) [4].

The hacker community has some give on the symmetry reason; thus, it tolerates licenses like the Netscape Public License (NPL) that give some profit privileges to the originators of the code (specifically in the NPL case, the exclusive right to use the open-source Mozilla code in derivative products including closed source). It has less give on the unintended-consequences reason, and none at all on preserving the option to fork (which is why Sun's Java and Jini Sun Community Source License schemes have been largely rejected by the community).

(It bears repeating here that nobody in the hacker community *wants* projects to split into competing development lines; indeed, as I observed in *Homesteading the Noosphere*, there is very strong social pressure against forking, for good reasons. Nobody wants to be on a picket line, in court, or in a firefight either. But the right to fork is like the right to strike, the right to sue, or the right to bear arms—you don't want to have to exercise any of these rights, but it's a signal of serious danger when anyone tries to take them away.)

These reasons explain the clauses of the Open Source Definition, which was written to express the consensus of the hacker community regarding the critical features of the standard licenses (the GPL, the BSD license, the MIT License, and the Artistic License). These clauses have the effect (though not the intention) of making direct sale value very hard to capture.

INDIRECT SALE-VALUE MODELS

Nevertheless, there are ways to make markets in software-related services that capture something like indirect sale value. There are five known and two speculative models of this kind (more may be developed in the future).

LOSS-LEADER/MARKET POSITIONER

In this model, you use open-source software to create or maintain a market position for proprietary software that generates a direct revenue stream. In the most common variant, open-source client software enables sales of server software, or subscription/advertising revenue associated with a portal site.

Netscape Communications, Inc. was pursuing this strategy when it open-sourced the Mozilla browser in early 1998. The browser side of their business was at 13% of revenues and dropping when Microsoft first shipped Internet Explorer (IE). Intensive marketing of IE (and shady bundling practices that would later become the central issue of an antitrust lawsuit) quickly ate into Netscape's browser market share, creating concern that Microsoft intended to monopolize the browser market and then use defacto control of HTML and HTTP to drive Netscape out of the server market.

By open-sourcing the still widely popular Netscape browser, Netscape effectively denied Microsoft the possibility of a browser monopoly. They expected that open-source collaboration would accelerate the development and debugging of the browser, and hoped that Microsoft's IE would be reduced to playing catch-up and prevented from exclusively defining HTML.

This strategy worked. In November 1998 Netscape actually began to regain business-market share from IE. By the time Netscape was acquired by AOL in early 1999, the competitive advantage of keeping Mozilla in play was sufficiently clear that one of AOL's first public commitments was to continue supporting the Mozilla project, even though it was still in alpha stage.

WIDGET FROSTING

This model is for hardware manufacturers (hardware, in this context, includes anything from Ethernet or other peripheral boards all the way up to entire computer systems). Market pressures have forced hardware companies to write and maintain software (from device drivers through configuration tools all the way up to the level of entire operating systems), but the software itself is not a profit center. It's an overhead—often a substantial one.

In this situation, opening source is a no-brainer. There's no revenue stream to lose, so there's no downside. What the vendor gains is a dramatically larger developer pool, more rapid and flexible response to customer needs, and better reliability through peer review. It gets ports to other environments for free. It probably also gains increased customer loyalty as its customers' technical staffs put increasing amounts of time into the code to improve the source as they require.

There are a couple of vendor objections commonly raised specifically to open-sourcing hardware drivers. Rather than mix these objections with discussion of more general issues here, I have written specifically on this topic (see **UNKNOWN XREF**).

The 'future-proofing' effect of open source is particularly strong with respect to widget frosting. Hardware products have a finite production and support lifetime; after that, the customers are on their own. But if they have access to driver source and can patch those drivers as needed, they're more likely to be happier repeat customers.

A very dramatic example of adopting the widget frosting model was Apple Computer's decision in mid-March 1999 to open-source "Darwin", the core of their Mac OS X server operating system.

GIVE AWAY THE RECIPE, OPEN A RESTAURANT

In this model, one open-sources software to create a market position not for closed software (as in the loss-leader/market-positioner case) but for services.

(I used to call this "Give Away the Razor, Sell Razor Blades", but the coupling is not really as close as the razor/razor-blade analogy implies.)

This model was first used by Cygnus Solutions, arguably the first open-source business (1989). At the time, the GNU tools provided a common development environment across several machines, but each tool used a different configuration process and required a different set of patches to run on each platform. Cygnus domesticated the GNU tools and created the "configure" script to unify the build process (the recipe), and then sold support services and binaries bundled with their version of the GNU tools (the restaurant). In accordance with the GPL, they permitted customers to freely use, distribute, and modify the software that they distributed, but the service contract could be terminated (or a higher fee had to be paid) if there were more users at the site using the support services than were accounted for in the contract (no sharing at the salad bar).

This also is what Red Hat and other Linux distributors do. What they are actually selling is not the software, the bits itself, but the value added by assembling and testing a running operating system that is warranted (if only implicitly) to be merchantable and to be plug-compatible with other operating systems carrying the same brand. Other elements of their value proposition include free installation support and the provision of options for continuing support contracts.

The market-building effect of open source can be extremely powerful, especially for companies that are inevitably in a service position to begin with. One very instructive recent case is Digital Creations, a website-design house started up in 1998 that specializes in complex database and transaction sites. Their major tool, the intellectual-property crown jewels of the company, is an object publisher that has been through several names and incarnations but is now called Zope.

When the Digital Creations people went looking for venture capital, the venture capitalist they brought in carefully evaluated their prospective market niche, their people, and their tools. The VC then recommended that Digital Creations take Zope open-source.

By traditional software industry standards, this looks like an absolutely crazy move. Conventional business school wisdom has it that core intellectual property like Zope is a company's crown jewels, never under any circumstances to be given away. But the VC had two related insights. One is that Zope's true core asset is actually the brains and skills of its people. The second is that Zope is likely to generate more value as a market-builder than as a secret tool.

To see this, compare two scenarios. In the conventional one, Zope remains Digital Creations's secret weapon. Let's stipulate that it's a very effective one. As a result, the firm will be able to deliver superior quality on short schedules—*but nobody knows that.* It will be easy to satisfy customers, but harder to build a customer base to begin with.

The VC, instead, saw that open-sourcing Zope could be critical advertising for Digital Creations's *real* asset—its people. He expected that customers evaluating Zope would consider it more efficient to hire the experts than to develop in-house Zope expertise.

One of the Zope principals has since confirmed very publicly that their open-source strategy has "opened many doors we wouldn't have got in otherwise" [*sic*]. Potential customers do indeed respond to the logic of the situation—and Digital Creations, accordingly, is prospering.

Another up-to-the-minute example is e-smith, inc. (*http://www.e-smith.net/*). This company sells support contracts for turnkey Internet server software that is open-source, a customized Linux. One of the principals, describing the spread of free downloads of e-smith's software, says "Most companies would consider that software piracy; we consider it free marketing" (*http://www.globetechnology.com/gam/News/19990625/BAND.html*).

ACCESSORIZING

In this model, you sell accessories for open-source software. At the low end, mugs and T-shirts; at the high end, professionally edited and produced documentation.

O'Reilly & Associates, Inc., publishers of many excellent reference volumes on open-source software, is a good example of an accessorizing company. O'Reilly actually hires and supports well-known open-source hackers (such as Larry Wall and Brian Behlendorf) as a way of building its reputation in its chosen market.

FREE THE FUTURE, SELL THE PRESENT

In this model, you release software in binaries and source with a closed license, but one that includes an expiration date on the closure provisions. For example, you might write a license that permits free redistribution, forbids commercial use without fee, and guarantees that the software come under GPL terms a year after release or if the vendor folds.

Under this model, customers can ensure that the product is customizable to their needs, because they have the source. The product is future-proofed—the license guarantees that an open source community can take over the product if the original company dies.

Because the sale price and volume are based on these customer expectations, the original company should enjoy enhanced revenues from its product versus releasing it with an exclusively closed-source license. Furthermore, as older code is GPLed, it will get serious peer review, bug fixes, and minor features, which removes some of the 75% maintainance burden on the originator.

This model has been successfully pursued by Aladdin Enterprises, makers of the popular Ghostscript program (a PostScript interpreter that can translate to the native languages of many printers).

The main drawback of this model is that the closure provisions tend to inhibit peer review and participation early in the product cycle, precisely when they are needed most.

Free the Software, Sell the Brand

This is a speculative business model. You open-source a software technology, retain a test suite or set of compatibility criteria, then sell users a brand certifying that their implementation of the technology is compatible with all others wearing the brand.

(This is how Sun Microsystems ought to be handling Java and Jini.)

Update: In July 2000, Sun announced that it would open-source its Star Office, and that they would be selling the use of the Star Office brand to lines of development of that codebase that pass Sun's validation suite.

Free the Software, Sell the Content

This is another speculative business model. Imagine something like a stock-ticker subscription service. The value is neither in the client software nor the server but in providing objectively reliable information. So you open-source all the software and sell subscriptions to the content. As hackers port the client to new platforms and enhance it in various ways, your market automatically expands.

(This is why AOL ought to open-source its client software.)

When to Be Open, When to Be Closed

Having reviewed business models that support open-source software development, we can now approach the general question of when it makes economic sense to be open-source and when to be closed-source. First, we must be clear what the payoffs are from each strategy.

WHAT ARE THE PAYOFFS?

The closed-source approach allows you to collect rent from your secret bits; on the other hand, it forecloses the possibility of truly independent peer review. The open-source approach sets up conditions for independent peer review, but you don't get rent from your secret bits.

The payoff from having secret bits is well understood; traditionally, software business models have been constructed around it. Until recently, the payoff from independent peer review was not well understood. The Linux operating system, however, drives home a lesson that we should probably have learned years ago from the history of the Internet's core software and other branches of engineering—that open-source peer review is the only scalable method for achieving high reliability and quality.

In a competitive market, therefore, customers seeking high reliability and quality will reward software producers who go open-source and discover how to maintain a revenue stream in the service, value-add, and ancilliary markets associated with software. This phenomenon is what's behind the astonishing success of Linux, which came from nowhere in 1996 to be the second-most-popular operating system in the business server market by mid-2000 (and some surveys actually showed it passing Microsoft's share in late 2000). In early 1999 IDC projected that Linux would grow faster than all other operating systems combined through 2003; this projection has held true so far.

An almost equally important payoff of open source is its utility as a way to propagate open standards and build markets around them. The dramatic growth of the Internet owes much to the fact that nobody owns TCP/IP; nobody has a proprietary lock on the core Internet protocols.

The network effects behind TCP/IP's and Linux's success are fairly clear and reduce ultimately to issues of trust and symmetry—potential parties to a shared infrastructure can rationally trust it more if they can see how it works all the way down, and will prefer an infrastructure in which all parties have symmetrical rights to one in which a single party is in a privileged position to extract rents or exert control.

It is not, however, actually necessary to assume network effects in order for symmetry issues to be important to software consumers. No software consumer will rationally choose to lock itself into a supplier-controlled monopoly by becoming dependent on closed source if any open-source alternative of acceptable quality is available. This argument gains force as the software becomes more critical to the software consumer's business—the more vital it is, the less the consumer can tolerate having it controlled by an outside party.

There's a flip side to this. Economists know that, in general, asymmetric information makes markets work poorly. Higher-quality goods get driven out when it's more lucrative to collect rent on privileged information than it is to invest in producing better products. In general, not just in software, secrecy is the enemy of quality.

Finally, an important customer payoff of open-source software related to the trust issue is that it's future-proof. If sources are open, the customer has some recourse if the vendor goes belly-up. This may be particularly important for widget frosting, since hardware tends to have short life cycles, but the effect is more general and translates into increased value for all kinds of open-source software.

How Do They Interact?

When the rent from secret bits is higher than the return from open source, it makes economic sense to be closed-source. When the return from open source is higher than the rent from secret bits, it makes sense to go open source.

In itself, this is a trivial observation. It becomes nontrivial when we notice that the payoff from open source is harder to measure and predict than the rent from secret bits—and that said payoff is grossly underestimated much more often than it is overestimated. Indeed, until the mainstream business world began to rethink its premises following the Mozilla source release in early 1998, the open-source payoff was incorrectly but very generally assumed to be zero.

So how can we evaluate the payoff from open source? It's a difficult question in general, but we can approach it as we would any other predictive problem. We can start from observed cases where the open-source approach has succeeded or failed. We can try to generalize to a model that gives at least a qualitative feel for the contexts in which open source is a net win for the investor or business trying to maximize returns. We can then go back to the data and try to refine the model.

From the analysis presented in *The Cathedral and the Bazaar*, we can expect that open source has a high payoff where (a) reliability/stability/scalability are critical, and (b) correctness of design and implementation is not readily verified by means other than independent peer review. (The second criterion is met in practice by most non-trivial programs.)

A consumer's rational desire to avoid being locked into a monopoly supplier will increase its interest in open source (and, hence, the competitive-market value for suppliers of going open) as the software becomes more critical to that consumer. Thus, another criterion (c) pushes towards open source when the software is a business-critical capital good (as, for example, in many corporate MIS departments).

As for application area, we observed above that open-source infrastructure creates trust and symmetry effects that, over time, will tend to attract more customers and to outcompete closed-source infrastructure; and it is often better to have a smaller piece of such a rapidly-expanding market than a bigger piece of a closed and stagnant one. Accordingly, for infrastructure software, an open-source play for ubiquity is quite likely to have a higher long-term payoff than a closed-source play for rent from intellectual property.

In fact, the ability of potential customers to reason about the future consequences of vendor strategies and their reluctance to accept a supplier monopoly implies a stronger constraint; without already having overwhelming market power, you can choose either an open-source ubiquity play or a direct-revenue-from-closed-source play—but not both. (Analogues of this principle are visible elsewhere—e.g., in electronics markets where customers often refuse to buy sole-source designs.) The case can be put less negatively: where network effects (positive network externalities) dominate, open source is likely to be the right thing.

We may sum up this logic by observing that open source seems to be most successful in generating greater returns than is closed source in software that (d) establishes or enables a common computing and communications infrastructure.

Finally, we may note that purveyors of unique or just highly differentiated services have more incentive to fear the copying of their methods by competitors than do vendors of services for which the critical algorithms and knowledge bases are well understood. Accordingly, open source is more likely to dominate when (e) key methods (or functional equivalents) are part of common engineering knowledge.

The Internet core software, Apache, and Linux's implementation of the standard Unix API are prime exemplars of all five criteria. The path towards open source in the evolution of such markets are well-illustrated by the reconvergence of data networking on TCP/IP in the mid-1990s following 15 years of failed attempts at empire-building with closed protocols such as DECNET, XNS, IPX, and the like.

On the other hand, open source seems to make the least sense for companies that have unique possession of a value-generating software technology (strongly fulfilling criterion (e)), which is (a) relatively insensitive to failure, which can (b) readily be verified by means other than independent peer review, which is not (c) business-critical, and which would not have its value substantially increased by (d) network effects or ubiquity.

As an example of this extreme case, in early 1999 I was asked "Should we go open source?" by a company that writes software to calculate cutting patterns for sawmills that want to extract the maximum yardage of planks from logs. My conclusion was "No." The only criterion this comes even close to fulfilling is (c); but in a pinch, an experienced operator could generate cut patterns by hand.

Note that my answer night have been very different if the cut-pattern calculator had been written by a sawmill-equipment manufacturer. In that case, opening the code would have increased the value of the associated hardware they were selling. Also note that if some open-source cut-pattern calculator already existed (perhaps the one written by the sawmill-equipment manufacturer) the closed-source product would have trouble competing with it—not so much for reasons of price, but because customers would perceive on open-source advantage in customizability and other traits.

An important point is that where a particular product or technology sits on these scales may change over time, as we'll see in the following case study.

In summary, the following discriminators push towards open source:

1. Reliability/stability/scalability are critical.
2. Correctness of design and implementation cannot readily be verified by means other than independent peer review.
3. The software is critical to the user's control of his/her business.
4. The software establishes or enables a common computing and communications infrastructure.
5. Key methods (or functional equivalents of them) are part of common engineering knowledge.

Doom: A Case Study

The history of id software's best-selling game Doom illustrates ways in which market pressure and product evolution can critically change the payoff magnitudes for closed versus open source.

When Doom was first released in late 1993, its first-person, real-time animation made it utterly unique (the antithesis of criterion (e)). Not only was the visual impact of the techniques stunning (far exceeding the flat-world animation in its predecessor Wolfenstein 3D), but for many months nobody could figure out how it had been achieved on the underpowered microprocessors of that time. These secret bits were worth some very serious rent. In addition, the potential payoff from open source was low. As a solo game, the software (a) incurred tolerably low costs on failure, (b) was not tremendously hard to verify, (c) was not business-critical for any consumer, and (d) did not benefit from network effects. It was economically rational for Doom to be closed source.

However, the market around Doom did not stand still. Would-be competitors invented functional equivalents of its animation techniques, and other "first-person shooter" games like Duke Nukem began to appear. As these games ate into Doom's market share, the value of the rent from secret bits went down.

On the other hand, efforts to expand that share brought on new technical challenges—better reliability, more game features, a larger user base, and multiple platforms. With the advent of multiplayer "deathmatch" play and Doom gaming services, the market began to display substantial network effects. All this was demanding programmer-hours that id would have preferred to spend on the next game.

From the time the game was first released, id had looked benignly on the publication of technical specs that helped people to create data objects for the game, and occasionally cooperated directly with hackers by answering specific questions or publishing an existing specs document of their own. They also encouraged the Internet distribution of new Doom data.

The technical and market trends raised the payoff from opening the source; Doom's opening of specifications and encouragement of third-party add-ons increased the perceived value of the game and created a secondary market for them to exploit. At some point the payoff curves crossed over and it became economically rational for id to shift to making money in that secondary market (with products such as game-scenario anthologies) and then open up the Doom source. Sometime after this point, it actually happened. The full source for Doom was released in late 1997.

KNOWING WHEN TO LET GO

Doom makes an interesting case study because it is neither an operating system nor communications/networking software; it is thus far removed from the usual and obvious examples of open-source success. Indeed, Doom's life cycle, complete with crossover point, may be coming to typify that of applications software in today's code ecology—one in which communications and distributed computation both create serious robustness/reliability/scalability problems only addressible by peer review, and frequently cross boundaries both between technical environments and between competing actors (with all the trust and symmetry issues that implies).

Doom evolved from solo to deathmatch play. Increasingly, the network effect *is* the computation. Similar trends are visible even in the heaviest business applications, such as ERP systems, as businesses network ever more intensively with suppliers and customers—and, of course, they are implicit in the whole architecture of the World Wide Web. It follows that almost everywhere, the open-source payoff is steadily increasing.

If present trends continue, the central challenge of software technology and product management in the next century will be knowing when to let go—when to allow closed code to pass into the open-source infrastructure in order to exploit the peer-review effect and capture higher returns in service and other secondary markets.

There are obvious revenue incentives not to miss the crossover point too far in either direction. Beyond that, there's a serious opportunity risk in waiting too long—you could get scooped by a competitor going open-source in the same market niche.

The reason this is a serious issue is that both the pool of users and the pool of talent available to be recruited into open-source cooperation for any given product category is limited, and recruitment tends to stick. If two producers are the first and second to open-source competing code of roughly equal function, the first is likely to attract the most users and the most and best-motivated co-developers; the second will have to take leavings. Recruitment tends to stick, as users gain familiarity and developers sink time investments in the code itself.

Open Source as a Strategic Weapon

Sometimes, open-sourcing can be effective not just as a way to grow markets but as a strategic maneuver against a company's competition. It will be fruitful to re-examine some of the business tactics described above from that angle; not directly as revenue generators but as ways to break into and reshape markets.

COST-SHARING AS A COMPETITIVE WEAPON

Earlier, we considered Apache as an example of better and cheaper infrastructure development through cost-sharing in an open-source project. For software and systems vendors competing against Microsoft and its IIS web server, the Apache project is also a competitive weapon. It would be difficult, perhaps impossible, for any other single web server vendor to completely offset the advantages of Microsoft's huge war chest and desktop-monopoly market power. But Apache enables each corporate participant in the project to offer a web server that is both technically superior to IIS and reassures customers with a majority market share—at far lower cost. This improves the market position and cost of production for value-added electronic-commerce products (like IBM's WebSphere).

This generalizes. Open, shared infrastructure gives its participants competitive advantages. One is lower cost per participant to produce salable products and services. Another is a market position that reassures customers that they are much less likely to be stuck with orphaned technology as a result of one vendor's change in strategy or tactics.

RESETTING THE COMPETITION

When the development of the open-source X window system was funded by DEC in the 1980s, their explicit goal was to "reset the competition". At the time there were several competing alternative graphics environments for Unix in play, notably including Sun Microsystems' NeWS system. DEC strategists believed (probably correctly) that if Sun were able to establish a proprietary graphics standard it would get a lock on the booming Unix-workstation market. By funding X and lending it engineers, and by allying with many smaller vendors to establish X as a *defacto* standard, DEC was able to neutralize advantages held by Sun and other competitors with more in-house expertise in graphics. This moved the focus of competition in the workstation market towards hardware, where DEC was historically strong.

This too generalizes. Open source is attractive to smart customers, and to potential allies not large enough to fund competive development on their own. An open-source project, pitched at the right time, can do better than just competing successfully against closed-source alternatives; it can actually prevent them from getting traction in the marketplace, resetting the competition and redirecting it from an area where the initiating company is weak to one where it is strong.

GROWING THE POND

Red Hat Software funded the development of the RPM packaging system in order to give the Linux world a standard binary package installer. By doing so, they bet that the increased confidence such a standard installer would give potential customers would be worth more in future revenue than either the development cost of the software or the revenue potentially lost to competitors also able to use it.

Sometimes the smartest way to become a bigger frog is to make the pond grow faster. This, of course, is the economic reason technology firms have participated in public standards—and it's useful to think of open-source software as an executable standard. Besides being an excellent market builder, this strategy can be a direct competitive weapon when a small company uses it to offset the mass and market power of a much larger company outside the standards-based alliance. In Red Hat's case, the obvious and acknowledged big competitor is Microsoft; standardization on RPM across most Linux distributions went a significant way towards neutralizing advantages Microsoft had previously held in ease of system administration on its Windows machines.

PREVENTING A CHOKEHOLD

In explaining the previous loss-leader/market-positioner business model, I described how Netscape's open-sourcing of the Mozilla browser was a (successful) maneuver aimed at preventing Microsoft from effectively locking up HTML markup and the HTTP protocol.

Often, it's more important to prevent your competition from getting a chokehold on a particular technology than it is to control the technology yourself. By open-sourcing, you greatly increase the potential size of your blocking coalition.

OPEN SOURCE AND STRATEGIC BUSINESS RISK

Ultimately, the reasons open source seems destined to become a widespread practice have more to do with customer demand and market pressures than with supply-side efficiencies for vendors. I have already discussed, from the vendor's point of view, the effects of customer demand for reliability and for infrastructure with no single dominant player, and how these have played out historically in the evolution of networking. There is more to be said, though, about the behavior of customers in a market where open source is a factor.

Put yourself for the moment in the position of a CTO at a Fortune 500 corporation contemplating a build or upgrade of your firm's IT infrastructure. Perhaps you need to choose a network operating system to be deployed enterprise-wide; perhaps your concerns involve 24/7 web service and e-commerce; perhaps your business depends on being able to field high-volume, high-reliability transaction databases.

Suppose you go the conventional closed-source route. If you do, then you put your firm at the mercy of a supplier monopoly— because by definition, there is only one place you can go for support, bug fixes, and enhancements. If the supplier doesn't perform, you will have no effective recourse because you are effectively locked in by your initial investment and training costs. Your supplier knows this. Under these circumstances, do you suppose the software will change to meet *your* needs and *your* business plan ... or your *supplier's* needs and your *supplier's* business plan?

The brutal truth is this: when your key business processes are executed by opaque blocks of bits that you can't even see inside (let alone modify), *you have lost control of your business.* You need your supplier more than your supplier needs you—and you will pay, and pay, and pay again for that power imbalance. You'll pay in higher prices, you'll pay in lost opportunities, and you'll pay in lock-in that grows worse over time as the supplier (who has refined its game on a lot of previous victims) tightens its hold.

Contrast this with the open-source choice. If you go that route, *you have the source code,* and no one can take it away from you. Instead of a supplier monopoly with a chokehold on your business, you now have multiple service companies bidding for your business—and you not only get to play them against each other, you have the option of building your own captive support organization if that looks less expensive than contracting out. The market works for *you.*

The logic is compelling; depending on closed-source code is an unacceptable strategic business risk. So much so that I believe it will not be very long until closed-source single-vendor acquisitions when there is an open-source alternative available will be viewed as actual fiduciary irresponsibility, and rightly grounds for a shareholder lawsuit.

THE BUSINESS ECOLOGY
OF OPEN SOURCE

The open-source community has organized itself in a way that tends to amplify the productivity effects of open source. In the Linux world, in particular, it's an economically significant fact that there are multiple competing Linux distributors that form a tier separate from the developers.

Developers write code, and make the code available over the Internet. Each distributor selects some subset of the available code, integrates and packages and brands it, and sells it to customers. Users choose among distributions, and may supplement a distribution by downloading code directly from developer sites.

The effect of this tier separation is to create a very fluid internal market for improvements. Developers compete with each other, for the attention of distributors and users, on the quality of their software. Distributors compete for user dollars on the appropriateness of their selection policies, and on the value they can add to the software.

A first-order effect of this internal market structure is that no node in the net is indispensible. Developers can drop out; even if their portion of the code base is not picked up directly by some other developer, the competition for attention will tend to rapidly generate functional alternatives. Distributors can fail without damaging or compromising the common open-source code base. The ecology as a whole has a more rapid response to market demands, and more capability to resist shocks and regenerate itself, than any monolithic vendor of a closed-source operating system can possibly muster.

Another important effect is to lower overhead and increase efficiency through specialization. Developers don't experience the pressures that routinely compromise conventional closed projects and turn them into tar-pits—no lists of pointless and distracting check-list features from Marketing, no management mandates to use inappropriate and outdated languages or development environments, no requirement to reinvent wheels in a new and incompatible way in the name of product differentiation or intellectual-property protection, and (most importantly) *no deadlines*. No rushing a 1.0 out the door before it's done right. De Marco and Lister observed in their discussion of the "wake me when it's over" management style in "Peopleware: Productive Projects and Teams"⁵ that this generally conduces not only to higher quality but actually to the most rapid delivery of a working result.

Distributors, on the other hand, get to specialize in the things distributors can do most effectively. Freed of the need to fund massive and ongoing software development just to stay competitive, they can concentrate on system integration, packaging, quality assurance, and service.

Both distributors and developers are kept honest by the constant feedback from and monitoring by users that is an integral part of the open-source method.

Coping with Success

The "Tragedy of the Commons" may not be applicable to open-source development as it happens today, but that doesn't mean there are not any reasons to wonder if the present momentum of the open-source community is sustainable. Will key players defect from cooperation as the stakes become higher?

There are several levels on which this question can be asked. Our "Comedy of the Commons" counter-story is based on the argument that the value of individual contributions to open source is hard to monetize. But this argument has much less force for firms (like, say, Linux distributors) that already have a revenue stream associated with open source. Their contribution is already being monetized every day. Is their present cooperative role stable?

Examining this question will lead us to some interesting insights about the economics of open-source software in the real world of present time—and about what a true service-industry paradigm implies for the software industry in the future.

On the practical level, applied to the open-source community as it exists now, this question is usually posed in one of two different ways. One: will Linux fragment? Two: conversely, will Linux develop a dominant, quasi-monopolistic player?

The historical analogy many people turn to when considering if Linux will fragment is the behavior of the proprietary-Unix vendors in the 1980s. Despite endless talk of open standards, despite numerous alliances and consortia and agreements, proprietary Unix fell apart. The vendors' desire to differentiate their products by adding and modifying operating-system facilities proved stronger than their interest in growing the total size of the Unix market by maintaining compatibility (and consequently lowering both entry barriers for independent software developers and total cost of ownership for consumers).

This is quite unlikely to happen to Linux, for the simple reason that all the distributors are constrained to operate from a common base of open source code. It's not really possible for any one of them to maintain differentiation, because the licenses under which Linux code are developed effectively require them to share code with all parties. The moment any distributor develops a feature, all competitors are free to clone it.

Since all parties understand this, nobody even thinks about doing the kinds of maneuvers that fragmented proprietary Unix. Instead, Linux distributors are forced to compete in ways that actually *benefit* the consumer and the overall market. That is, they must compete on service, on support, and their design bets on what interfaces actually conduce to ease installation and use.

The common source base also forecloses the possibility of monopolization. When Linux people worry about this, the name usually muttered is "Red Hat", that of the largest and most successful of the distributors (with somewhere around 90% estimated market share in the U.S.). But it is notable that within days after the May 1999 announcement of Red Hat's long-awaited 6.0 release—before Red Hat's CD-ROMs actually shipped in any quantity—CD-ROM images of the release built from Red Hat's own public FTP site were being advertised by a book publisher and several other CD-ROM distributors at lower prices than Red Hat's expected list price.

Red Hat itself didn't turn a hair at this, because its founders understand very clearly that they do not and cannot own the bits in their product; the social norms of the Linux community forbid that. In a latter-day take on John Gilmore's famous observation that the Internet interprets censorship as damage and routes around it, it has been aptly said that the hacker community responsible for Linux interprets attempts at control as damage and routes around them. For Red Hat to have protested the pre-release cloning of its newest product would have seriously compromised its ability to elicit future cooperation from its developer community.

Perhaps more importantly in present time, the software licenses that express these community norms in a binding legal form actively forbid Red Hat from monopolizing the sources of the code on which their product is based. The only thing they can sell is a brand/service/support relationship with people who are freely willing to pay for that. This is not a context in which the possibility of a predatory monopoly looms very large.

OPEN R&D AND THE REINVENTION OF PATRONAGE

There is one other respect in which the infusion of real money into the open-source world is changing it. The community's stars are increasingly finding they can get paid for what they want to do, instead of pursuing open source as a hobby funded by another day job. Corporations like Red Hat, O'Reilly & Associates, and VA Linux Systems are building what amount to semi-independent research arms with charters to hire and maintain stables of open-source talent.

This makes economic sense only if the cost per head of maintaining such a lab can easily be paid out of the expected gains it will achieve by growing the firm's market faster. O'Reilly can afford to pay the leaders of Perl and Apache to do their thing because it expects their efforts will enable it to sell more Perl- and Apache-related books and draw more people to its conferences. VA Linux Systems can fund its laboratory branch because improving Linux boosts the use value of the workstations and servers it sells. And Red Hat funds Red Hat Advanced Development Labs to increase the value of its Linux offering and attract more customers.

To strategists from more traditional sectors of the software industry, reared in cultures that regard patent- or trade-secret–protected intellectual property as the corporate crown jewels, this behavior may (despite its market-growing effect) seem inexplicable. Why fund research that every one of your competitors is (by definition) free to appropriate at no cost?

There seem to be two controlling reasons. One is that as long as these companies remain dominant players in their market niches, they can expect to capture a proportional lion's share of the returns from the open research and development. Using R&D to buy future profits is hardly a novel idea; what's interesting is the implied calculation that the expected future gains are sufficiently large that these companies can readily tolerate free riders in order to get the peer-review effect.

While this obvious expected-future–value analysis is a necessary one in a world of hard-nosed capitalists keeping their eyes on return-on-investment, it is not actually the most interesting mode of explanation for star-hiring, because the firms themselves advance a fuzzier one. They will tell you if asked that they are simply doing the right thing by the community they come from. Your humble author is sufficiently well-acquainted with principals at all three of the firms cited above to testify that these protestations cannot be dismissed as humbug. Indeed, I was personally recruited onto the board of VA Linux Systems in late 1998 explicitly so that I would be available to advise them on "the right thing", and have found them far from unwilling to listen when I did so.

An economist is entitled to ask what payoff is involved here. If we accept that talk of doing the right thing is not empty posturing, we should next inquire what self-interest of the firm the "right thing" serves. Nor is the answer, in itself, either surprising or difficult to verify by asking the right questions. As with superficially altruistic behavior in other industries, what these firms actually believe they're buying is goodwill.

Working to earn goodwill, and valuing it as an asset predictive of future market gains, is hardly novel either. What's interesting is the extremely high valuation that the behavior of these firms suggests they put on that goodwill. They're demonstrably willing to hire expensive talent for projects that are not direct revenue generators even during the most capital-hungry phases of the runup to IPO. And, at least so far, the market has richly rewarded this behavior.

The principals of these companies themselves are quite clear about the reasons why goodwill is especially valuable to them. They rely heavily on volunteers among their customer base both for product development and as an informal marketing arm. Their relationship with their customer base is intimate, often relying on personal trust bonds between individuals within and outside the firm. They do not merely use the hacker community; they identify with it.

These observations reinforce a lesson we learned earlier from a different line of reasoning. The intimate relationship between Red Hat/VA/O'Reilly and their customers/developers is not one typical of manufacturing firms. Rather, it carries to an interesting extreme the patterns characteristic of highly professionalized and knowledge-intensive service industries. Looking outside the technology industry, we can see these patterns in (for example) law firms, medical practices, and universities.

We may observe, in fact, that open-source firms hire star hackers for much the same reasons that universities hire star academics. In both cases, the practice is similar in mechanism and effect to the system of aristocratic patronage that funded most fine art until after the Industrial Revolution—a similarity of which some parties are fully aware.

GETTING THERE FROM HERE

The market mechanisms for funding (and making a profit from!) open-source development are still evolving rapidly. The business models we've reviewed in this essay probably will not be the last to be invented. Investors are still thinking through the consequences of reinventing the software industry as one with an explicit focus on service rather than closed intellectual property, and will be for some time to come.

This conceptual revolution will have some cost in foregone profits for people investing in the sale-value 5% of the industry; historically, service businesses are not as lucrative as manufacturing businesses (though as any doctor or lawyer could tell you, the return to the actual practitioners is often higher). Any foregone profits, however, will be more than matched by benefits on the cost side, as software consumers reap tremendous savings and efficiencies from open-source products. (There's a parallel here to the effects that the displacement of the traditional voice-telephone network by the Internet is having everywhere).

The promise of these savings and efficiencies is creating a market opportunity that entrepreneurs and venture capitalists are now moving in to exploit. As the first draft of this essay was in preparation, Silicon Valley's most prestigious venture-capital firm took a lead stake in the first startup company to specialize in 24/7 Linux technical support (Linuxcare). In August 1999 Red Hat's IPO was (despite a background slump in Internet and technology stocks) wildly successful. It is generally expected that several Linux- and open-source–related IPOs will be floated before the end of 1999 —and that they too will be quite successful. (Year 2000 update: they were!)

Another very interesting development is the beginnings of systematic attempts to make task markets in open-source development projects. SourceXchange (*http://www.sourcexchange.com/process.html*) and CoSource (*http://www.cosource.com/*) represent slightly different ways of trying to apply a reverse-auction model to funding open-source development.

The overall trends are clear. We mentioned before IDC's projection that Linux will grow faster than all other operating systems *combined* through 2003. Apache is at 61% market share and rising steadily. Internet usage is exploding, and surveys such as the Internet Operating System Counter (*http://leb.net/hzo/ioscount/*) show that Linux and other open-source operating systems are already a plurality on Internet hosts and steadily gaining share against closed systems. The need to exploit open-source Internet infrastructure increasingly conditions not merely the design of other software but the business practices and software use/purchase patterns of every corporation there is. These trends, if anything, seem likely to accelerate.

CONCLUSION: LIFE AFTER THE REVOLUTION

What will the world of software look like once the open-source transition is complete?

Some programmers worry that the transition to open source will abolish or devalue their jobs. The standard nightmare is what I call the "Open-Source Doomsday" scenario. This starts with the market value of software going to zero because of all the free source code out there. Use value alone doesn't attract enough consumers to support software development. The commercial software industry collapses. Programmers starve or leave the field. Doomsday arrives when the open-source culture itself (dependent on the spare time of all these pros) collapses, leaving nobody around who can program competently. All die. Oh, the embarrassment!

We have already observed a number of sufficient reasons this won't happen, starting with the fact that most developers' salaries don't depend on software sale value in the first place. But the very best one, worth emphasizing here, is this: when did you last see a software development group that didn't have way more than enough work waiting for it? In a swiftly changing world, in a rapidly complexifying and information-centered economy, there will always be plenty of work and a healthy demand for people who can make computers do things—no matter how much time and how many secrets they give away.

For purposes of examining the software market itself, it will be helpful to sort kinds of software by how completely the service they offer is describable by open technical standards, which is well correlated with how commoditized the underlying service has become.

This axis corresponds reasonably well to what people are normally thinking when they speak of 'applications' (not at all commoditized, weak or nonexistent open technical standards), 'infrastructure' (commoditized services, strong standards), and 'middleware' (partially commoditized, effective but incomplete technical standards). The paradigm cases today in 2000 would be a word processor (application), a TCP/IP stack (infrastructure), and a database engine (middleware).

The payoff analysis we did earlier suggests that infrastructure, applications, and middleware will be transformed in different ways and exhibit different equilibrium mixes of open and closed source. It also suggested the prevalence of open source in a particular software area would be a function of whether substantial network effects operate there, what the costs of failure are, and to what extent the software is a business-critical capital good.

We can venture some predictions if we apply these heuristics not to individual products but to entire segments of the software market. Here we go:

Infrastructure (the Internet, the Web, operating systems, and the lower levels of communications software that has to cross boundaries between competing parties) will be almost all open source, cooperatively maintained by user consortia and by for-profit distribution/service outfits with a role like that of Red Hat today.

Applications, on the other hand, will have the most tendency to remain closed. There will be circumstances under which the use value of an undisclosed algorithm or technology will be high enough (and the costs associated with unreliability will be low enough, and the risks associated with a supplier monopoly sufficiently tolerable) that consumers will continue to pay for closed software. This is likeliest to remain true in standalone vertical-market applications where network effects are weak. Our lumber-mill example earlier is one such; biometric identification software seems likeliest, of 1999's hot prospects, to be another.

Middleware (like databases, development tools, or the customized top ends of application protocol stacks) will be more mixed. Whether middleware categories tend to go closed or open seems likely to depend on the cost of failures, with higher cost creating market pressure for more openness.

To complete the picture, however, we need to notice that neither 'applications' nor 'middleware' are really stable categories. Earlier we saw that individual software technologies seem to go through a natural life cycle from rationally closed to rationally open. The same logic applies in the large.

Applications tend to fall into middleware as standardized techniques develop and portions of the service are commoditized. (Databases, for example, became middleware after SQL decoupled frontends from engines.) As middleware services are commoditized, they will in turn tend to fall into the open-source infrastructure—a transition we're seeing in operating systems right now.

In a future that includes competition from open source, we can expect that the eventual destiny of any software technology will be to either die or become part of the open infrastructure itself. While this is hardly happy news for entrepreneurs who would like to collect rent on closed software forever, it does suggest that the software industry as a whole will *remain* entrepreneurial, with new niches constantly opening up at the upper (application) end and a limited lifespan for closed-IP monopolies as their product categories fall into infrastructure.

Finally, of course, this equilibrium will be great for the software consumers who are driving the process. More and more high-quality software will become permanently available to use and build on instead of being discontinued or locked in somebody's vault. Ceridwen's magic cauldron is, finally, too weak a metaphor—because food is consumed or decays, whereas software sources potentially last forever. The free market, in its widest libertarian sense including *all* un-coerced activity whether trade or gift, can produce perpetually increasing software wealth for everyone.

AFTERWORD: WHY CLOSING A DRIVERS LOSES ITS VENDOR MONEY

Manufacturers of peripheral hardware (Ethernet cards, disk controllers, video board and the like) have historically been reluctant to open up. This is changing now, with players like Adaptec and Cyclades beginning to routinely disclose specifications and driver source code for their boards. Nevertheless, there is still resistance out there. In this appendix I attempt to dispel several of the economic misconceptions that sustain it.

If you are a hardware vendor, you may fear that open-sourcing may reveal important things about how your hardware operates that competitors could copy, thus gaining an unfair competitive advantage. Back in the days of three- to five-year product cycles this was a valid argument. Today, the time your competitors' engineers would need to spend copying and understanding the copy is a damagingly large portion of the product cycle, time they are *not* spending innovating or differentiating their own product.

This is not a new insight. Former KGB chief Oleg Kalugin puts the case well (*http://cnn.com/SPECIALS/cold.war/experience/spies/interviews/kalugin/*):

> For instance, when we stole IBMs in our blueprints, or some other electronic areas which the West made great strides in and we were behind, it would take years to implement the results of our intelligence efforts. By that time, in five or seven years, the West would go forward, and we would have to steal again and again, and we'd fall behind more and more.

But Rudyard Kipling put it better in his poem The Mary Gloster (*http://www.everypoet.com/archive/poetry/Rudyard_Kipling/kipling_the_mary_gloster.htm*), nearly a century ago. He wrote:

> And they asked me how I did it,
>   and I gave 'em the Scripture text,
> "You keep your light so shining
>   a little in front o' the next!"
> They copied all they could follow,
>   but they couldn't copy my mind,
> And I left 'em sweating and stealing
>   a year and a half behind.

Acceleration to Internet time makes this effect bite harder. If you're really ahead of the game, plagiarism is a trap you *want* your competitors to fall into!

In any case, these details don't stay hidden for long these days. Hardware drivers are not like operating systems or applications; they're small, easy to disassemble, and easy to clone. Even teenage novice programmers can do this—and frequently do.

There are literally thousands of Linux and FreeBSD programmers out there with both the capability and the motivation to build drivers for a new board. For many classes of device that have relatively simple interfaces and well-known standards (such as disk controllers and network cards) these eager hackers can often prototype a driver almost as rapidly your own shop could, even without documentation and without disassembling an existing driver.

Even for tricky devices like video and sound cards, there is not much you can do to thwart a clever programmer armed with a disassembler. Costs are low and legal barriers are porous; Linux is an international effort and there is always a jurisdiction in which reverse-engineering will be legal.

For hard evidence that all these claims are true, examine the list of devices supported in the Linux kernel and notice the rate at which new ones are added to the kernel even without vendor support.

Another good reason to open your drivers is so that you can *concentrate* on innovation. Imagine no longer having to spend your internal staff's time and salaries on rewriting, testing, and distributing new binaries for each new kernel as it comes out. You certainly have better things to do with all that skill.

Yet another good reason: nobody wants to wait six months for bug fixes. If you have any open-source competition at all, they are likely to bury you for this reason alone.

Of course, there's the future-proofing effect previously referred to. Customers want open source because they know it will extend the lifetime of the hardware beyond the point that it is cost-effective for you to support it.

The best reason, though, is because selling hardware is what makes money for you. There is no market demand for your secrecy; in fact, quite the reverse. If your drivers are hard to find, if they have to be updated frequently, if they (worst of all) run poorly, it reflects badly on your hardware and you will sell less of it. Open source can solve these problems and boost your revenues.

The message? Keeping your driver secret looks attractive in the short run, but is probably bad strategy in the long run (certainly when you're competing with other vendors that are already open). But if you must do it, burn the code into an onboard ROM. Then publish the interface to the ROM. Go open as much as possible to build your market and demonstrate to potential customers that you believe in your capacity to out-think and out-innovate competitors where it matters.

If you stay closed you will usually get the worst of all worlds—your secrets will still get exposed, you won't get free development help, and you won't have wasted your stupider competition's time on cloning. Most importantly, you miss an avenue to widespread early adoption. A large and influential market (the people who manage the servers that run effectively all of the Internet and a plurality of all business data centers) will correctly write your company off as clueless and defensive because you didn't realize these things. Then they'll buy their boards from someone who did.

REVENGE OF THE HACKERS

✦ ✦ ✦

The eruption of open-source software into the main-stream in 1998 was the revenge of the hackers after 20 years of marginalization. I found myself semi-accidentally cast as chief rabble-rouser and propagandist. In this essay, I describe the tumultuous year that followed, focusing on the media stategy and language we used to break through to the Fortune 500. I finish with a look at where the trend curves are going.

REVENGE OF THE HACKERS

I wrote the first version of *A Brief History of Hackerdom* in 1996 as a web resource. I had been fascinated by hacker culture *as a* culture for many years, since long before I edited the first edition of *The New Hacker's Dictionary* in 1990. By late 1993, many people (including myself) had come to think of me as the hacker culture's tribal historian and resident ethnographer. I was comfortable in that role.

At that time, I had not the faintest idea that my amateur anthropologizing could itself become a significant catalyst for change. I think nobody was more surprised than I when that happened. But the consequences of that surprise are still reverberating through the hacker culture and the technology and business worlds today.

In this essay, I'll recapitulate from my personal point of view the events that immediately led up to the January 1998 "shot heard 'round the world" of the open-source revolution. I'll reflect on the remarkable distance we've come since. Then I will tentatively offer some projections into the future.

BEYOND BROOKS'S LAW

My first encounter with Linux came in late 1993, via the pioneering Yggdrasil CD-ROM distribution. By that time, I had already been involved in the hacker culture for 15 years. My earliest experiences had been with the primitive ARPAnet of the late 1970s; I was even briefly a tourist on the ITS machines. I had already been writing free software and posting it to Usenet before the Free Software Foundation was launched in 1984, and was one of the FSF's first contributors. I had just published the second edition of *The New Hacker's Dictionary*. I thought I understood the hacker culture—and its limitations—pretty well.

As I have written elsewhere, encountering Linux came as a shock. Even though I had been active in the hacker culture for many years, I still carried in my head the unexamined assumption that hacker amateurs, gifted though they might be, could not possibly muster the resources or skill necessary to produce a usable multitasking operating system. The HURD developers, after all, had been evidently failing at this for a decade.

But where they failed, Linus Torvalds and his community succeeded. And they did not merely fulfill the minimum requirements of stability and functioning Unix interfaces. No. They blew right past that criterion with exuberance and flair, providing hundreds of megabytes of programs, documents, and other resources. Full suites of Internet tools, desktop-publishing software, graphics support, editors, games . . . you name it.

Seeing this feast of wonderful code spread in front of me as a working system was a much more powerful experience than merely knowing, intellectually, that all the bits were probably out there. It was as though for years I'd been sorting through piles of disconnected car parts—only to be suddenly confronted with those same parts assembled into a gleaming red Ferrari, door open, keys swinging from the lock, and engine gently purring with a promise of power . . . .

The hacker tradition I had been observing for two decades seemed suddenly alive in a vibrant new way. In a sense, I had already been made part of this community, for several of my personal free-software projects had been added to the mix. But I wanted to get in deeper . . . because every delight I saw also deepened my puzzlement. It was too good!

The lore of software engineering is dominated by Brooks's Law, articulated in Fred Brooks's classic *The Mythical Man-Month*.

Brooks predicts that as your number of programmers N rises, work performed scales as N but complexity and vulnerability to bugs rises as N^2. N^2 tracks the number of communications paths (and potential code interfaces) between developers' code bases.

Brooks's Law predicts that a project with thousands of contributors ought to be a flaky, unstable mess. Somehow the Linux community had beaten the N^2 effect and produced an OS of astonishingly high quality. I was determined to understand how they did it.

It took me three years of participation and close observation to develop a theory, and another year to test it experimentally. And then I sat down and wrote *The Cathedral and the Bazaar* to explain what I had seen.

MEMES AND MYTHMAKING

What I saw around me was a community that had evolved the most effective software-development method ever *and didn't know it!* That is, an effective practice had evolved as a set of customs, transmitted by imitation and example, without the theory or language to explain why the practice worked.

In retrospect, lacking that theory and that language hampered us in two ways. First: we couldn't think systematically about how to improve our own methods. Second: we couldn't explain or sell the method to anyone else.

At the time, I was thinking about only the first effect. My sole intention in writing the original paper was to give the hacker culture an appropriate language to use internally, to explain itself to itself. So I wrote down what I had seen, framed as a narrative and with appropriately vivid metaphors to describe the logic that could be deduced behind the customs.

There was no really fundamental discovery in *The Cathedral and the Bazaar*. I did not invent any of the methods it describes. What was novel was not the facts it described but those metaphors and the narrative—a simple, powerful story that encouraged the reader to see the facts in a new way. I was attempting a bit of memetic engineering on the hacker culture's generative myths.

I first gave the full paper at Linux Kongress, May 1997 in Bavaria. The fact that it was received with rapt attention and thunderous applause by an audience in which there were very few native speakers of English seemed to confirm that I was onto something. But, as it turned out, the sheer chance that I was seated next to publisher Tim O'Reilly at the Thursday night banquet set in motion a more important train of consequences.

As a long-time admirer of O'Reilly's institutional style, I had been looking forward to meeting Tim for some years. We had a wide-ranging conversation (much of it exploring our common interest in classic science fiction) that led to an invitation for me to deliver *The Cathedral and the Bazaar* at Tim's Perl Conference later in the year.

Once again, the paper was well-received—with cheers and a standing ovation, in fact. I knew from my email that since Bavaria, word about *The Cathedral and the Bazaar* had spread over the Internet like a fire in dry grass. Many in the audience had already read it, and my speech was less a revelation of novelty for them than an opportunity to celebrate the new language and the consciousness that went with it. That standing ovation was not so much for my work as for the hacker culture itself—and rightly so.

Though I didn't know it, my experiment in memetic engineering was about to light a bigger fire. Some of the people for whom my speech was genuinely novel were from Netscape Communications, Inc. And Netscape was in trouble.

Netscape, a pioneering Internet-technology company and Wall Street highflier, had been targeted for destruction by Microsoft. Microsoft rightly feared that the open Web standards embodied by Netscape's browser might lead to an erosion of the Redmond giant's lucrative monopoly on the PC desktop. All the weight of

Microsoft's billions, and shady tactics that would later trigger an antitrust lawsuit, were deployed to crush the Netscape browser.

For Netscape, the issue was less browser-related income (never more than a small fraction of their revenues) than maintaining a safe space for their much more valuable server business. If Microsoft's Internet Explorer achieved market dominance, Microsoft would be able to bend the Web's protocols away from open standards and into proprietary channels that only *Microsoft's* servers would be able to service.

Within Netscape there was intense debate about how to counter the threat. One of the options proposed early on was to throw the Netscape browser source open—but it was a hard case to argue without strong reasons to believe that doing so would prevent Internet Explorer dominance.

I didn't know it at the time, but *The Cathedral and the Bazaar* became a major factor in making that case. Through the winter of 1997, as I was working on the material for my next paper, the stage was being set for Netscape to break the rules of the proprietary game and offer my tribe an unprecedented opportunity.

THE ROAD TO MOUNTAIN VIEW

On 22 January 1998 Netscape announced that it would release the sources of the Netscape client line to the Internet. Shortly after the news reached me the following day, I learned that CEO Jim Barksdale was describing my work to national-media reporters as "fundamental inspiration" for the decision.

This was the event that commentators in the computer trade press would later call "the shot heard 'round the world'—and Barksdale had cast me as its Thomas Paine, whether I wanted the role or not. For the first time in the history of the hacker culture, a Fortune 500 darling of Wall Street had bet its future on the belief that *our way was right*. And, more specifically, that *my analysis* of "our way" was right.

This is a pretty sobering kind of shock to deal with. I had not been very surprised when *The Cathedral and the Bazaar* altered the hacker culture's image of itself; that was the result I had been trying for, after all. But I was astonished (to say the least) by the news of its success on the outside. So I did some very hard thinking in first few hours after word reached me. About the state of Linux and the hacker community. About Netscape. And about whether I, personally, had what it would take to make the next step.

It was not difficult to conclude that helping Netscape's gamble succeed had just become a very high priority for the hacker culture, and thus for me personally. If Netscape's gamble failed, we hackers would probably find all the opprobrium of that failure piled on our heads. We'd be discredited for another decade. And that would be just too much to take.

By this time I had been in the hacker culture, living through its various phases, for twenty years. Twenty years of repeatedly watching brilliant ideas, promising starts, and superior technologies crushed by slick marketing. Twenty years of watching hackers dream and sweat and build, too often only to watch the likes of the bad old IBM or the bad new Microsoft walk away with the real-world prizes. Twenty years of living in a ghetto—a fairly comfortable ghetto full of interesting friends, but still one walled in by a vast and intangible barrier of mainsteam prejudice inscribed "ONLY FLAKES LIVE HERE".

The Netscape announcement cracked that barrier, if only for a moment; the business world had been jolted out of its complacency about what 'hackers' are capable of. But lazy mental habits have huge inertia. If Netscape failed, or perhaps even if they succeeded, the experiment might come to be seen as a unique one-off not worth trying to repeat. And then we'd be back in the same ghetto, walls higher than before.

To prevent that, we needed Netscape to succeed. So I considered what I had learned about bazaar-mode development, and called up Netscape, and offered to help with developing their license and in working out the details of the strategy. In early February I flew to Mountain View at their request for seven hours of meetings with various groups at Netscape HQ, and helped them develop the outline of what would become the Mozilla Public License and the Mozilla organization.

While there, I met with several key people in the Silicon Valley and national Linux community. While helping Netscape was clearly a short-term priority, everybody I spoke with had already understood the need for some longer-term strategy to follow up on the Netscape release. It was time to develop one.

THE ORIGINS OF 'OPEN SOURCE'

It was easy to see the outlines of the strategy. We needed to take the pragmatic arguments I had pioneered in *The Cathedral and the Bazaar*, develop them further, and push them hard, in public. Because Netscape itself had an interest in convincing investors that its strategy was not crazy, we could count on it to help the promotion. We also recruited Tim O'Reilly (and through him, O'Reilly & Associates) very early on.

The real conceptual breakthrough, though, was admitting to ourselves that what we needed to mount was in effect a *marketing campaign*—and that it would require marketing techniques (spin, image-building, and rebranding) to make it work.

Hence the term 'open source', which the first participants in what would later become the Open Source campaign (and, eventually, the Open Source Initiative organization) invented at a meeting held in Mountain View in the offices of VA Research (now VA Linux Systems) on 3 February 1998.

It seemed clear to us in retrospect that the term 'free software' had done our movement tremendous damage over the years. Part of this stemmed from the fact that the word 'free' has two different meanings in the English language, one suggesting a price of zero and one related to the idea of liberty. Richard Stallman, whose Free Software Foundation has long championed the term, says "Think free speech, not free beer" but the ambiguity of the term has nevertheless created serious problems—especially since most free software is also distributed free of charge.

Most of the damage, though, came from something worse—the strong association of the term 'free software' with hostility to intellectual property rights, communism, and other ideas hardly likely to endear it to an MIS manager.

It was, and still is, beside the point to argue that the Free Software Foundation is not hostile to all intellectual property and that its position is not exactly communistic. We knew that. What we realized, under the pressure of the Netscape release, was that FSF's actual position didn't matter. Only the fact that its evangelism had backfired (associating 'free software' with these negative stereotypes in the minds of the trade press and the corporate world) actually mattered.

Our success after Netscape would depend on replacing the negative FSF stereotypes with *positive* stereotypes of our own—pragmatic tales, sweet to managers' and investors' ears, of higher reliability and lower cost and better features.

In conventional marketing terms, our job was to rebrand the product, and build its reputation into one the corporate world would hasten to buy.

Linus Torvalds endorsed the idea the day after that first meeting. We began acting on it within a few days after. Bruce Perens had the *opensource.org* domain registered and the first version of the Open Source website (*http://www.opensource.edu*) up within a week. He also suggested that the Debian Free Software Guidelines become the 'Open Source Definition' (*http://www.opensource.org/osd.html*), and began the process of registering 'Open Source' as a certification mark so that we could legally require people to use 'Open Source' for products conforming to the OSD.

Even the particular tactics needed to push the strategy seemed pretty clear to me at this early stage (and were explicitly discussed at the initial meeting). Key themes follow.

1. FORGET BOTTOM-UP; WORK ON TOP-DOWN

One of the things that seemed clearest was that the historical Unix strategy of bottom-up evangelism (relying on engineers to persuade their bosses by rational argument) had been a failure. This was naive and easily trumped by Microsoft. Further, the Netscape breakthrough didn't happen that way. It happened because a strategic decision-maker (Jim Barksdale) got the clue and then imposed that vision on the people below him.

The conclusion was inescapable. Instead of working bottom-up, we should be evangelizing top-down—making a direct effort to capture the CEO/CTO/CIO types.

2. LINUX IS OUR BEST DEMONSTRATION CASE

Promoting Linux must be our main thrust. Yes, there are other things going on in the open-source world, and the campaign will bow respectfully in their direction—but Linux started with the best name recognition, the broadest software base, and the largest developer community. If Linux can't consolidate the breakthrough, nothing else will, pragmatically speaking, have a prayer.

3. CAPTURE THE FORTUNE 500

There are other market segments that spend more dollars (small business and home office being the most obvious examples) but those markets are diffuse and hard to address. The Fortune 500 doesn't merely *have* lots of money, it concentrates lots of money where it's relatively accessible. Therefore, the software industry largely does what the Fortune 500 business market tells it to do. And therefore, it is primarily the Fortune 500 we need to convince.

4. Co-opt the Prestige Media that Serve the Fortune 500

The choice to target the Fortune 500 implies that we need to capture the media that shape the climate of opinion among top-level decision-makers and investors: very specifically, the *New York Times*, the *Wall Street Journal*, the *Economist*, *Forbes*, and *Barron's Magazine*.

On this view, co-opting the technical trade press is necessary but not sufficient; it's important essentially as a pre-condition for storming Wall Street itself via the elite mainstream media.

5. Educate Hackers in Guerrilla Marketing Tactics

It was also clear that educating the hacker community itself would be just as important as mainstream outreach. It would be insufficient to have one or a handful of ambassadors speaking effective language if, at the grass roots, most hackers were making arguments that didn't work.

6. Use the Open Source Certification Mark to Keep Things Pure

One of the threats we faced was the possibility that the term 'open source' would be "embraced and extended" by Microsoft or other large vendors, corrupting it and losing our message. It is for this reason the Bruce Perens and I decided early on to register the term as a certification mark and tie it to the Open Source Definition (a copy of the Debian Free Software Guidelines). This would allow us to scare off potential abusers with the threat of legal action.

It eventually developed that the U.S. Patent and Trademark office would not issue a trademark for such a descriptive phrase. Fortunately, by the time we had to write off the effort to formally trademark "Open Source" a year later, the term had acquired its own momentum in the press and elsewhere. The sorts of serious abuse we feared have not (at least, not yet as of November 2000) actually materialized.

THE ACCIDENTAL REVOLUTIONARY

Planning this kind of strategy was relatively easy. The hard part (for me, anyway) was accepting what my own role had to be.

One thing I understood from the beginning is that the press almost completely tunes out abstractions. They won't write about ideas without larger-than-life personalities fronting them. Everything has to be story, drama, conflict, sound bites. Otherwise, most reporters will simply go to sleep—and even if they don't, their editors will.

Accordingly, I knew somebody with very particular characteristics would be needed to front the community's response to the Netscape opportunity. We needed a firebrand, a spin doctor, a propagandist, an ambassador, an evangelist—somebody who could dance and sing and shout from the housetops and seduce reporters and huggermug with CEOs and bang the media machine until its contrary gears ground out the message: *the revolution is here!*

Unlike most hackers, I have the brain chemistry of an extrovert and had already had extensive experience at dealing with the press. Looking around me, I couldn't see anyone better qualified to play evangelist. But I didn't want the job, because I knew it would cost me my life for many months, maybe for years. My privacy would be destroyed. I'd probably end up both caricatured as a geek by the mainstream press and (worse) despised as a sell-out or glory-hog by a significant fraction of my own tribe. Worse than all the other bad consequences put together, I probably wouldn't have time to hack anymore!

I had to ask myself: are you fed up enough with watching your tribe lose to do *whatever it takes* to win? I decided the answer was yes—and having so decided, threw myself into the dirty but necessary job of becoming a public figure and media personality.

I'd learned some basic media chops while editing *The New Hacker's Dictionary*. This time I took it much more seriously and developed an entire theory of media manipulation, which I then proceeded to apply. The theory centers around the use of what I call "attractive dissonance" to fan an itchy curiosity about the evangelist, and then exploiting that itch for all it's worth in promoting the ideas.

This is not the place for a detailed exposition of my theory. But intelligent readers can probably deduce much of it from the phrase "optimal level of provocation" and the fact that my interview technique involves cheerfully discussing my interests in guns, anarchism, and witchcraft while looking as well-groomed, boyishly charming, and all-American wholesome as I can possibly manage. The trick is to sound challengingly weird but convey a reassuring aura of honesty and simplicity. (Note that to make the trick work, I think you have to genuinely *be* like that; faking either quality has a high risk of exposure and I don't recommend it.)

The combination of the "open source" label and deliberate promotion of myself as an evangelist turned out to have both the good and bad consequences that I expected. The ten months after the Netscape announcement featured a steady exponential increase in media coverage of Linux and the open-source world in general. Throughout this period, approximately a third of these articles quoted me directly; most of the other two thirds used me as a background source. At the same time, a vociferous minority of hackers declared me an evil egotist. I managed to preserve a sense of humor about both outcomes (though occasionally with some difficulty).

My plan from the beginning was that, eventually, I would hand off the evangelist role to some successor, either an individual or organization. There would come a time when charisma became less effective than broad-based institutional respectability (and, from my own point of view, the sooner the better!). I am attempting to transfer my personal connections and carefully built-up reputation with the press to the Open Source Initiative, an incorporated nonprofit formed specifically to manage the Open Source trademark. At time of writing I am the president of this organization, but hope and expect not to remain so indefinitely.

PHASES OF THE CAMPAIGN

The open-source campaign began with the Mountain View meeting, and rapidly collected an informal network of allies over the Internet (including key people at Netscape and O'Reilly & Associates). Where I write "we" below I'm referring to that network.

From 3 February to around the time of the actual Netscape release on 31 March, our primary concern was convincing the hacker community that the 'open source' label and the arguments that went with it represented our best shot at persuading the mainstream. As it turned out, the change was rather easier than we expected. We discovered a lot of pent-up demand for a message less doctrinaire than the Free Software Foundation's.

Tim O'Reilly invited 20-odd leaders of major free software projects to what came to be called the Free Software Summit on 7 March. When these leaders voted to adopt the term 'open source', they formally ratified a trend that was already clear at the grass roots among developers. By six weeks after the Mountain View meeting, a healthy majority of the community was speaking our language.

The publicity following the Free Software Summit introduced the mainstream press to the term, and also gave notice that Netscape was not alone in adopting the open-source concept. We'd given a name to a phenomenon whose impact was already larger than anyone outside the Internet community had yet realized. Far from being fringe challengers, open source programs were already market leaders in providing key elements of the Internet infrastructure. Apache was the leading web server, with more than 50% market share (now grown to more than 60%). Perl was the dominant programming language for the new breed of web-based applications. Sendmail routes more than 80% of all Internet email messages. And even the ubiquitous domain name system (which lets us use names like *www.yahoo.com* rather than obscure numeric IP addresses) depends almost entirely on an open-source program called BIND. As Tim O'Reilly said during the press conference following the summit, pointing to the assembled programmers and project leaders: "These people have created products with dominant market share using only the power of their ideas and the networked community of their co-developers." What more might be possible if large companies also adopted the open source methodology?

That was a good start to our 'air war', our attempt to change perceptions through the press. But we still needed to maintain momentum on the ground. In April, after the Summit and the actual Netscape release, our main concern shifted to recruiting as many open-source early adopters as possible. The goal was to make Netscape's move look less singular—and to buy us insurance in case Netscape executed poorly and failed its goals.

This was the most worrying time. On the surface, everything seemed to be coming up roses; Linux was moving technically from strength to strength, the wider open-source phenomenon was enjoying a spectacular explosion in trade press coverage, and we were even beginning to get positive coverage in the mainstream press. Nevertheless, I was uneasily aware that our success was still fragile. After an initial flurry of contributions, community participation in Mozilla was badly slowed down by its requirement for the proprietary Motif toolkit. None of the big independent software vendors had yet committed to Linux ports. Netscape was still looking lonely, and its browser still losing market share to

Internet Explorer. Any serious reverse could lead to a nasty back-lash in the press and public opinion.

Our first serious post-Netscape breakthrough came on 7 May when Corel Computer announced its Linux-based Netwinder net-work computer. But that wasn't enough in itself; to sustain the momentum, we needed commitments not from hungry second-stringers but from industry leaders. Thus, it was the mid-July announcements by Oracle and Informix that really closed out this vulnerable phase.

The database outfits joined the Linux party three months earlier than I expected, but none too soon. We had been wondering how long the positive buzz could last without major ISV support and feeling increasingly nervous about where we'd actually find that. After Oracle and Informix announced Linux ports other ISVs began announcing Linux support almost as a matter of routine, and even a failure of Mozilla became survivable.

Mid-July through the beginning of November was a consolidation phase. It was during this time that we started to see fairly steady coverage from the financial media I had originally targeted, led off by articles in the *Economist* and a cover story in *Forbes*. Various hardware and software vendors sent out feelers to the open-source community and began to work out strategies for getting advantage from the new model. And internally, the biggest closed-source ven-dor of them all was beginning to get seriously worried.

Just *how* worried became apparent when the now-infamous Halloween Documents (*http://www.opensource.org/halloween/*) leaked out of Microsoft. These internal strategy documents recog-nized the power of the open-source model, and outlined Microsoft's analysis of how to combat it by corrupting the open protocols on which open source depends and choking off cus-tomer choice.

The Halloween Documents were dynamite. They were a ringing testimonial to the strengths of open-source development from the company with the most to lose from Linux's success. And they confirmed a lot of people's darkest suspicions about the tactics Microsoft would consider in order to stop it.

The Halloween Documents attracted massive press coverage in the first few weeks of November. They created a new surge of interest in the open-source phenomenon, serendipitously confirming all the points we had been making for months. And they led directly to a request for me to confer with a select group of Merrill Lynch's major investors on the state of the software industry and the prospects for open source. Wall Street, finally, came to us.

The following six months were a study in increasingly surreal contrasts. On the one hand, I was getting invited to give talks on open source to Fortune 100 corporate strategists and technology investors; for the first time in my life, I got to fly first class and saw the inside of a stretch limousine. On the other hand, I was doing guerrilla street theater with grass-roots hackers—as in the riotously funny Windows Refund Day demonstration of 15 March 1999, when a band of Bay Area Linux users actually marched on the Microsoft offices in the glare of full media coverage, demanding refunds under the terms of the Microsoft End User License for the unused Windows software that had been bundled with their machines.

I knew I was going to be in town that weekend to speak at a conference hosted by the Reason Foundation, so I volunteered to be a marshal for the event. Back in December I'd been featured in a Star Wars parody plot (*http://www.userfriendly.org/cartoons/ archives/98dec/19981203.html*) in the Internet comic strip "User Friendly". So I joked with the organizers about wearing an Obi-Wan Kenobi costume at the demonstration.

To my surprise, when I arrived I found the organizers had actually made a passable Jedi costume—and that's how I found myself leading a parade that featured cheeky placards and an American flag and a rather large plastic penguin, booming out "May the Source be with you!" to delighted reporters. To my further surprise, I was drafted to make our statement to the press.

I suppose none of us should have really been astonished when the video made CNBC. The demonstration was a tremendous success. Microsoft's PR position, still trying to recover from the exposure of the Halloween Documents, took another body blow. And within weeks, major PC and laptop manufacturers began announcing that they would ship machines with no Windows installed and no "Microsoft tax" in the price. Our bit of guerilla theater, it appeared, had struck home.

THE FACTS ON THE GROUND

While the Open Source campaign's air war in the media was going on, key technical and market facts on the ground were also changing. I'll briefly review some of them here because they combine interestingly with the trends in press and public perception.

In the 18 months after the Netscape release, Linux continued to grow rapidly more capable. The development of solid SMP support and the effective completion of the 64-bit cleanup laid important groundwork for the future.

The roomful of Linux boxes used to render scenes for the Titanic threw a healthy scare of expensive graphics engines into builders. Then the Beowulf supercomputer-on-the-cheap project showed that Linux's Chinese-army sociology could be successfully applied even to cutting-edge scientific computing.

Nothing dramatic happened to vault Linux's open-source competitors into the limelight. And proprietary Unixes continued to lose market share; in fact, by mid-year only NT and Linux were actually gaining market share in the Fortune 500, and by late fall Linux was gaining faster (and more at the expense of NT than of other Unixes).

Apache continued to increase its lead in the web-server market. (By August 1999 Apache and its derivatives would be running fully 61% of the world's publicly accessible web servers.) In November 1998, Netscape's browser reversed its market-share slide and began to make gains against Internet Explorer.

In April 1999 the respected computer-market researchers IDG predicted that Linux would grow twice as fast as all other server operating systems combined through 2003—and faster than Windows NT. In May, Kleiner-Perkins (Silicon Valley's leading venture-capital firm) took a lead position in financing a Linux startup.

About the only negative development was the continuing problems of the Mozilla project. I have analyzed these elsewhere (in *The Magic Cauldron*). They came to a head when Jamie Zawinski, a Mozilla co-founder and the public face of the project, resigned a year and a day after the release of the source code, complaining of mismanagement and lost opportunities.

But it was an indication of the tremendous momentum open source had acquired by this time that Mozilla's troubles did not noticeably slow down the pace of adoption. The trade press, remarkably, drew the right lesson: "Open source," in Jamie's now-famous words, "is [great, but it's] not magic pixie dust."

In the early part of 1999 a trend began among big independent software vendors (ISVs) to port their business applications to Linux, following the lead set earlier by the major database vendors. In late July, the biggest of them all, Computer Associates, announced that it would be supporting Linux over much of its product line. And preliminary results from an August 1999 survey of 2000 IT managers revealed that 49% consider Linux an "important or essential" element of their enterprise computing strategies. Another survey by IDC described what it called "an amazing level of growth" since 1998, when the market research couldn't find statistically significant use of Linux; 13% of the respondents now employ it in business operations.

The year 1999 also saw a wave of wildly successful Linux IPOs by Red Hat Linux, VA Linux Systems, and other Linux companies. While the overblown dot-com–like initial valuations investors originally put on them didn't outlast the big market corrections in March 2000, these firms established an unmistakable for-profit industry around open source that continues to be a focus of investor interest.

INTO THE FUTURE

I have rehearsed recent history here only partly to get it into the record. More importantly, it sets a background against which we can understand near-term trends and project some things about the future.

First, safe predictions for the next year:

- The open-source developer population will continue to explode, a growth fueled by ever-cheaper PC hardware and fast Internet connections.

- Linux will continue to lead the way, the sheer size of its developer community overpowering the higher average skill of the open-source BSD people and the tiny HURD crew.

- ISV commitments to support the Linux platform will increase dramatically; the database-vendor commitments were a turning point.

- The Open Source campaign will continue to build on its victories and successfully raise awareness at the CEO/CTO/CIO and investor level. MIS directors will feel increasing pressure to go with open-source products not from below but from *above*.

- Stealth deployments of Samba-over-Linux will replace increasing numbers of NT machines even at shops that have all-Microsoft policies.

- The market share of proprietary Unixes will continue to gradually erode. At least one of the weaker competitors (likely
  DG-UX or HP-UX) will actually fold. But by the time it happens, analysts will attribute it to Linux's gains rather than
  Microsoft's.

- Microsoft will not have an enterprise-ready operating system,
  because Windows 2000 will not ship in a usable form. (At 60
  million lines of code and still bloating, its development is out
  of control.)

I wrote the above predictions in mid-December of 1998. All are
still holding good as of November 2000, two years after they were
written. Only the last one is arguable; Microsoft managed to ship
Windows 2000 by drastically curtailing its feature list; adoption
rates have not been what they hoped.

Extrapolating these trends certainly suggests some slightly riskier
predictions for the medium term (18 to 32 months out).

- Support operations for commercial customers of open-source
  operating systems will become big business, both feeding off
  of and fueling the boom in business use.

  (This has already come true in 1999 with the launch of Linux-
  Care, and Linux support-service announcements by IBM and
  HP and others.)

- Open-source operating systems (with Linux leading the way)
  will capture the ISP and business data-center markets. NT will
  be unable to resist this change effectively; the combination of
  low cost, open sources, and true 24/7 reliability will prove
  unstoppable.

- The proprietary-Unix sector will almost completely collapse.
  Solaris looks like a safe bet to survive on high-end Sun hardware, but most other players' proprietary Unixes will quickly
  become legacy systems.

  (In early 2000, SGI's IRIX was dead-ended by official Linux
  adoption within SGI itself, and in mid-2000 SCO agreed to be

acquired by Caldera. It now looks probable that a number of
Unix hardware vendors will switch horses to Linux without
much fuss, as SGI is already well into the process of doing.)

- Windows 2000 will be either canceled or dead on arrival.
  Either way it will turn into a horrendous train wreck, the
  worst strategic disaster in Microsoft's history. However, their
  marketing spin on this failure will be so deft that it will barely
  affect their hold on the consumer desktop within the next two
  years.

  (In mid-2000, a just-published IDG survey suggested that
  "dead on arrival" looks more likely all the time, with most
  large corporate respondents simply refusing to deploy the initial release and existing deployments experiencing serious
  security and stability problems. The fact that Microsoft itself
  was cracked twice in late October/early November of 2000
  hardly helped.)

At first glance, these trends look like a recipe for leaving Linux as
the last one standing. But life is not that simple, and Microsoft
derives such immense amounts of money and market clout from
the desktop market that it can't safely be counted out even after
the Windows 2000 train wreck.

But there are also reasons to believe that Microsoft is going to
experience serious problems in 2001 that aren't related to either
Linux or the Department of Justice. As hardware prices drop, the
59% of Microsoft's revenues that come from selling fixed-price
preinstallation licenses to PC OEMs is under pressure. Those fixed
license costs represent an ever-increasing slice of OEM's gross
margins; at some point, the OEMs are going to have to claw back
some of that last margin from Redmond in order to make any
profits at all. We know where the critical price point is from
observing the appliance and PDA market; it's at about $350 retail.
On previous trends, desktop prices will cross $350 going down
well before midyear 2001—and when that happens, OEMs will
have to defect from the Microsoft camp to survive.

Nor will it help Microsoft to respond in the obvious way by charging a percentage of the system's retail price instead of a fixed per-unit fee. OEMs can easily fiddle that system by unbundling expensive outboard components like the monitor—and even if they didn't, Wall Street would regard such a move as an admission that Microsoft had lost control of its future revenues. One way or another, Microsoft's revenues look likely to crash hard long before DOJ gets a final ruling.

So at two years out the crystal ball gets a bit cloudy. Which of several futures we get depends on questions like: will the DOJ actually succeed in breaking up Microsoft? Might BeOS or OS/2 or Mac OS/X or some other niche closed-source OS, or some completely new design, find a way to go open and compete effectively with Linux's 30-year-old base design? At least Y2K fizzled....

These are all fairly imponderable. But there is one such question that is worth pondering: Will the Linux community actually deliver a good end-user–friendly GUI interface for the whole system?

In the 1999 first edition of this book, I said the most likely scenario for late 2000/early 2001 has Linux in effective control of servers, data centers, ISPs, and the Internet, while Microsoft maintains its grip on the desktop. By November 2000 this prediction had proved out pretty completely except in large corporate data centers, and there it looks very likely to be fulfilled within months.

Where things go from there depend on whether GNOME, KDE, or some other Linux-based GUI (and the applications built or rebuilt to use it) ever get good enough to challenge Microsoft on its home ground.

If this were primarily a technical problem, the outcome would hardly be in doubt. But it isn't; it's a problem in ergonomic design and interface psychology, and hackers have historically been poor at these things. That is, while hackers can be very good at designing interfaces for other hackers, they tend to be poor at modeling the thought processes of the other 95% of the population well enough to write interfaces that J. Random End-User and his Aunt Tillie will pay to buy.

Applications were 1999's problem; it's now clear we'll swing enough ISVs to get the ones we don't write ourselves. I believe the problem for 2001 and later is whether we can grow enough to meet (and *exceed!*) the interface-design quality standard set by the Macintosh, combining that with the virtues of the traditional Unix way.

As of mid-2000, help may be on the way from the inventors of the Macintosh! Andy Hertzfeld and other members of the original Macintosh design team have formed an open-source company called Eazel with the explicit goal of bringing the Macintosh magic to Linux.

We half-joke about 'world domination', but the only way we will get there is by *serving* the world. That means J. Random End-User and his Aunt Tillie; and *that* means learning how to think about what we do in a fundamentally new way, and ruthlessly reducing the user-visible complexity of the default environment to an absolute minimum.

Computers are tools for human beings. Ultimately, therefore, the challenges of designing hardware and software must come back to designing for human beings—*all* human beings.

This path will be long, and it won't be easy. But I think the hacker community, in alliance with its new friends in the corporate world, will prove up to the task. And, as Obi-Wan Kenobi might say, "the Source will be with us".

BEYOND SOFTWARE?

✦ ✦ ✦

The essays in this book were a beginning, but they are not an end. There are many questions not yet resolved about open-source software. And there are many questions about other kinds of creative work and intellectual property that the open-source phenomenon raises, but does not really suggest a good answer for.

I am often asked if I believe the open-source model can be usefully applied to other kinds of goods than software. Most usually the question is asked about music, or the content of some kinds of books, or designs for computer and electronic hardware. Almost as frequently I am asked whether I think the open-source model has political implications.

I am not short of opinions about music, books, hardware, or politics. Some of those opinions do indeed touch on the ideas about peer review, decentralization, and openness explored in this book; the interested reader is welcome to visit my home site *http://www.tuxedo.org/~esr/* and make his or her own deductions. However, I have deliberately avoided such speculation in connection with my work as a theorist and ambassador of open source.

The principle is simple: *one battle at a time.* My tribe is waging a struggle to raise the quality and reliability expectations of software consumers and overturn the standard operating procedures of the software industry. We face entrenched opposition with a lot of money and mind-share and monopoly power. It's not an easy fight, but the logic and economics are clear; we can win and we will win. *If*, that is, we stay focused on that goal.

Staying focused on the goal involves not wandering down a lot of beguiling byways. This is a point I often feel needs emphasizing when I address other hackers, because in the past our representatives have shown a strong tendency to ideologize when they would have been more effective sticking to relatively narrow, pragmatic arguments.

Yes, the success of open source does call into some question the utility of command-and-control systems, of secrecy, of centralization, and of certain kinds of intellectual property. It would be almost disingenuous not to admit that it suggests (or at least harmonizes well with) a broadly libertarian view of the proper relationship between individuals and institutions.

These things having been said, however, it seems to me for the present more appropriate to try to avoid over-applying these ideas. A case in point; music and most books are not like software, because they don't generally need to be debugged or maintained. Without that requirement, the utility of peer review is much lower, and the rational incentives for some equivalent of open-sourcing therefore nearly vanish. I do not want to weaken the winning argument for open-sourcing software by tying it to a potential loser.

I expect the open-source movement to have essentially won its point about software within three to five years (that is, by 2003–2005). Once that is accomplished, and the results have been manifest for a while, they will become part of the background culture of non-programmers. At *that* point it will become more appropriate to try to leverage open-source insights in wider domains.

In the meantime, even if we hackers are not making an ideological noise about it, we will still be changing the world.

How to Become a Hacker

✦ ✦ ✦

Why This Document?

As editor of the Jargon File, *http://www.tuxedo.org/jargon/*, and author of a few other well-known documents of similar nature, I often get email requests from enthusiastic network newbies asking (in effect) "How can I learn to be a wizard hacker?" Oddly enough, there don't seem to be any FAQs or web documents that address this vital question, so here's mine.

If you are reading a snapshot of this document offline, the current version lives at *http://www.tuxedo.org/~esr/faqs/hacker-howto .html*.

Note: there is a list of Frequently Asked Questions at the end of this document [1]. Please read these—twice—before mailing me any questions about this document.

What Is a Hacker?

The Jargon File, *http://www.tuxedo.org/jargon/*, contains a bunch of definitions of the term 'hacker', most having to do with technical adeptness and a delight in solving problems and overcoming limits. If you want to know how to *become* a hacker, though, only two are really relevant.

There is a community, a shared culture, of expert programmers and networking wizards that traces its history back through decades to the first time-sharing minicomputers and the earliest ARPAnet experiments. The members of this culture originated the term 'hacker'. Hackers built the Internet. Hackers made the Unix operating system what it is today. Hackers run Usenet. Hackers make the World Wide Web work. If you are part of this culture, if you have contributed to it and other people in it know who you are and call you a hacker, you're a hacker.

The hacker mind-set is not confined to this software-hacker culture. There are people who apply the hacker attitude to other things, like electronics or music—actually, you can find it at the highest levels of any science or art. Software hackers recognize these kindred spirits elsewhere and may call them "hackers" too—and some claim that the hacker nature is really independent of the particular medium the hacker works in. But in the rest of this document we will focus on the skills and attitudes of software hackers, and the traditions of the shared culture that originated the term 'hacker'.

There is another group of people who loudly call themselves hackers, but aren't. These are people (mainly adolescent males) who get a kick out of breaking into computers and phreaking the phone system. Real hackers call these people 'crackers' and want nothing to do with them. Real hackers mostly think crackers are lazy, irresponsible, and not very bright, and object that being able to break security doesn't make you a hacker any more than being able to hotwire cars makes you an automotive engineer. Unfortunately, many journalists and writers have been fooled into using the word 'hacker' to describe crackers; this irritates real hackers to no end.

The basic difference is this: hackers build things, crackers break them.

If you want to be a hacker, keep reading. If you want to be a cracker, go read the alt.2600 (*news:alt.2600*) newsgroup and get ready to do five to ten in the slammer after finding out you aren't as smart as you think you are. And that's all I'm going to say about crackers.

The Hacker Attitude

Hackers solve problems and build things, and they believe in freedom and voluntary mutual help. To be accepted as a hacker, you have to behave as though you have this kind of attitude yourself. And to behave as though you have the attitude, you have to really believe the attitude.

But if you think of cultivating hacker attitudes as just a way to gain acceptance in the culture, you'll miss the point. Becoming the kind of person who believes these things is important for *you*— for helping you learn and keeping you motivated. As with all creative arts, the most effective way to become a master is to imitate the mind-set of masters—not just intellectually but emotionally as well.

So, if you want to be a hacker, repeat the following things until you believe them:

1. The world Is Full of Fascinating Problems Waiting to Be Solved.

Being a hacker is lots of fun, but it's a kind of fun that takes lots of effort. The effort takes motivation. Successful athletes get their motivation from a kind of physical delight in making their bodies perform, in pushing themselves past their own physical limits. Similarly, to be a hacker you have to get a basic thrill from solving problems, sharpening your skills, and exercising your intelligence.

If you aren't the kind of person who feels this way naturally, you'll need to become one in order to make it as a hacker. Otherwise you'll find your hacking energy is sapped by distractions like sex, money, and social approval.

(You also have to develop a kind of faith in your own learning capacity—a belief that even though you may not know all of what you need to solve a problem, if you tackle just a piece of it and learn from that, you'll learn enough to solve the next piece—and so on, until you're done.)

2. NOBODY SHOULD EVER HAVE TO SOLVE A PROBLEM TWICE.

Creative brains are a valuable, limited resource. They shouldn't be wasted on re-inventing the wheel when there are so many fascinating new problems waiting out there.

To behave like a hacker, you have to believe that the thinking time of other hackers is precious—so much so that it's almost a moral duty for you to share information, solve problems and then give the solutions away just so other hackers can solve *new* problems instead of having to perpetually re-address old ones.

(You don't have to believe that you're obligated to give *all* your creative product away, though the hackers that do are the ones who get most respect from other hackers. It's consistent with hacker values to sell enough of it to keep you in food and rent and computers. It's fine to use your hacking skills to support a family or even get rich, as long as you don't forget your loyalty to your art and your fellow hackers while doing it.)

3. BOREDOM AND DRUDGERY ARE EVIL.

Hackers (and creative people in general) should never be bored or have to drudge at stupid repetitive work, because when this happens it means they aren't doing what only they can do—solve new problems. This wastefulness hurts everybody. Therefore boredom and drudgery are not just unpleasant but actually evil.

To behave like a hacker, you have to believe this enough to want to automate away the boring bits as much as possible, not just for yourself but for everybody else (especially other hackers).

(There is one apparent exception to this. Hackers will sometimes do things that may seem repetitive or boring to an observer as a mind-clearing exercise, or in order to acquire a skill or have some particular kind of experience you can't have otherwise. But this is by choice—nobody who can think should ever be forced into a situation that bores them.)

4. Freedom Is Good.

Hackers are naturally anti-authoritarian. Anyone who can give you orders can stop you from solving whatever problem you're being fascinated by—and, given the way authoritarian minds work, will generally find some appallingly stupid reason to do so. So the authoritarian attitude has to be fought wherever you find it, lest it smother you and other hackers.

(This isn't the same as fighting all authority. Children need to be guided and criminals restrained. A hacker may agree to accept some kinds of authority in order to get something he wants more than the time he spends following orders. But that's a limited, conscious bargain; the kind of personal surrender authoritarians want is not on offer.)

Authoritarians thrive on censorship and secrecy. And they distrust voluntary cooperation and information-sharing—they only like 'cooperation' that they control. So to behave like a hacker, you have to develop an instinctive hostility to censorship, secrecy, and the use of force or deception to compel responsible adults. And you have to be willing to act on that belief.

5. Attitude Is No Substitute for Competence.

To be a hacker, you have to develop some of these attitudes. But copping an attitude alone won't make you a hacker, any more than it will make you a champion athlete or a rock star. Becoming a hacker will take intelligence, practice, dedication, and hard work.

Therefore, you have to learn to distrust attitude and respect competence of every kind. Hackers won't let poseurs waste their time, but they worship competence—especially competence at hacking, but competence at anything is good. Competence at demanding skills that few can master is especially good, and competence at demanding skills that involve mental acuteness, craft, and concentration is best.

If you revere competence, you'll enjoy developing it in yourself—the hard work and dedication will become a kind of intense play rather than drudgery. And that's vital to becoming a hacker.

BASIC HACKING SKILLS

The hacker attitude is vital, but skills are even more vital. Attitude is no substitute for competence, and there's a certain basic toolkit of skills that you have to have before any hacker will dream of calling you one.

This toolkit changes slowly over time as technology creates new skills and makes old ones obsolete. For example, it used to include programming in machine language, and didn't until recently involve HTML. But right now it pretty clearly includes the following.

1. LEARN HOW TO PROGRAM.

This, of course, is the fundamental hacking skill. If you don't know any computer languages, I recommend starting with Python. It is cleanly designed, well documented, and relatively kind to beginners. Despite being a good first language, it is not just a toy; it is very powerful and flexible and well suited for large projects. I have written a more detailed evaluation of Python, *http://noframes.linuxjournal.com/lj-issues/issue73/3882.html*. A tutorial is available at the Python website, *http://www.python.org*.

Java is also a good language for learning to program in. It is more difficult than Python, but produces faster code than Python. I think it makes an excellent second language.

But be aware that you won't reach the skill level of a hacker or even merely a programmer if you only know one or two languages—you need to learn how to think about programming problems in a general way, independent of any one language. To be a real hacker, you need to get to the point where you can learn a new language in days by relating what's in the manual to what you already know. This means you should learn several very different languages.

If you get into serious programming, you will have to learn C, the core language of Unix. C++ is very closely related to C; if you know one, learning the other will not be difficult. Neither language is a good one to try learning as your first, however.

Other languages of particular importance to hackers include Perl (*http://www.perl.com*) and LISP (*http://snaefell.tamu.edu/~colin/lp/*). Perl is worth learning for practical reasons; it's very widely used for active web pages and system administration, so that even if you never write Perl you should learn to read it. LISP is worth learning for the profound enlightenment experience you will have when you finally get it; that experience will make you a better programmer for the rest of your days, even if you never actually use LISP itself a lot.

It's best, actually, to learn all five of these (Python, Java, C/C++, Perl, and LISP). Besides being the most important hacking languages, they represent very different approaches to programming, and each will educate you in valuable ways.

I can't give complete instructions on how to learn to program here—it's a complex skill. But I can tell you that books and courses won't do it (many, maybe *most* of the best hackers are self-taught). You can learn language features—bits of knowledge—from books, but the mind-set that makes that knowledge into living skill can be learned only by practice and apprenticeship. What will do it is (a) *reading code* and (b) *writing code*.

Learning to program is like learning to write good natural language. The best way to do it is to read some stuff written by masters of the form, write some things yourself, read a lot more, write a little more, read a lot more, write some more . . . and repeat until your writing begins to develop the kind of strength and economy you see in your models.

Finding good code to read used to be hard, because there were few large programs available in source for fledgeling hackers to read and tinker with. This has changed dramatically; open-source software, programming tools, and operating systems (all built by hackers) are now widely available. Which brings me neatly to our next topic . . . .

2. Get One of the Open-Source Unixes and Learn to Use and Run It.

I'm assuming you have a personal computer or can get access to one (these kids today have it so easy :-)). The single most important step any newbie can take toward acquiring hacker skills is to get a copy of Linux or one of the BSD-Unixes, install it on a personal machine, and run it.

Yes, there are other operating systems in the world besides Unix. But they're distributed in binary—you can't read the code, and you can't modify it. Trying to learn to hack on a DOS or Windows machine or under MacOS is like trying to learn to dance while wearing a body cast.

Besides, Unix is the operating system of the Internet. While you can learn to use the Internet without knowing Unix, you can't be an Internet hacker without understanding Unix. For this reason, the hacker culture today is pretty strongly Unix-centered. (This wasn't always true, and some old-time hackers still aren't happy about it, but the symbiosis between Unix and the Internet has become strong enough that even Microsoft's muscle doesn't seem able to seriously dent it.)

So, bring up a Unix—I like Linux myself but there are other ways (and yes, you *can* run both Linux and DOS/Windows on the same machine). Learn it. Run it. Tinker with it. Talk to the Internet with it. Read the code. Modify the code. You'll get better programming tools (including C, LISP, Python, and Perl) than any

Microsoft operating system can dream of, you'll have fun, and you'll soak up more knowledge than you realize you're learning until you look back on it as a master hacker.

For more about learning Unix, see The Loginataka, *http://www.tuxedo.org/~esr/faqs/loginataka.html*.

To get your hands on a Linux, see the "Where can I get Linux" page, *http://linuxresources.com/apps/ftp.html*.

You can find BSD Unix help and resources at *http://www.bsd.org*.

(Note: I don't really recommend installing either Linux or BSD as a solo project if you're a newbie. For Linux, find a local Linux user's group and ask for help; or contact the Linux Internet Support Co-Operative, *http://www.linpeople.org*. LISC maintains IRC channels [*http://openprojects.nu/services/irc.html*] where you can get help.)

3. LEARN HOW TO USE THE WORLD WIDE WEB AND WRITE HTML.

Most of the things the hacker culture has built do their work out of sight, helping run factories and offices and universities without any obvious impact on how non-hackers live. The Web is the one big exception, the huge shiny hacker toy that even *politicians* admit is changing the world. For this reason alone (and a lot of other good ones as well) you need to learn how to work the Web.

This doesn't just mean learning how to drive a browser (anyone can do that), but learning how to write HTML, the Web's markup language. If you don't know how to program, writing HTML will teach you some mental habits that will help you learn. So build a home page.

But just having a home page isn't anywhere near good enough to make you a hacker. The Web is full of home pages. Most of them are pointless, zero-content sludge—very snazzy-looking sludge, mind you, but sludge all the same (for more on this see The HTML Hell Page: *http://www.tuxedo.org/~esr/html-hell.html*).

To be worthwhile, your page must have *content*—it must be interesting and/or useful to other hackers. And that brings us to the next topic....

STATUS IN THE HACKER CULTURE

Like most cultures without a money economy, hackerdom runs on reputation. You're trying to solve interesting problems, but how interesting they are, and whether your solutions are really good, is something that only your technical peers or superiors are normally equipped to judge.

Accordingly, when you play the hacker game, you learn to keep score primarily by what other hackers think of your skill (this is why you aren't really a hacker until other hackers consistently call you one). This fact is obscured by the image of hacking as solitary work; also by a hacker-cultural taboo (now gradually decaying but still potent) against admitting that ego or external validation are involved in one's motivation at all.

Specifically, hackerdom is what anthropologists call a *gift culture*. You gain status and reputation in it not by dominating other people, nor by being beautiful, nor by having things other people want, but rather by giving things away. Specifically, by giving away your time, your creativity, and the results of your skill.

There are basically five kinds of things you can do to be respected by hackers:

1. WRITE OPEN-SOURCE SOFTWARE

The first (the most central and most traditional) is to write programs that other hackers think are fun or useful, and give the program sources to the whole hacker culture to use.

(We used to call these works "free software", but this confused too many people who weren't sure exactly what "free" was supposed to mean. Many of us now prefer the term "open-source" software, *http://www.opensource.org/.*)

Hackerdom's most revered demigods are people who have written large, capable programs that met a widespread need and given them away, so that now everyone uses them.

2. Help Test and Debug Open-Source Software

They also serve who stand and debug open-source software. In this imperfect world, we will inevitably spend most of our software development time in the debugging phase. That's why any open-source author who's thinking will tell you that good beta-testers (who know how to describe symptoms clearly, localize problems well, can tolerate bugs in a quickie release, and are willing to apply a few simple diagnostic routines) are worth their weight in rubies. Even one of these can make the difference between a debugging phase that's a protracted, exhausting nightmare and one that's merely a salutary nuisance.

If you're a newbie, try to find a program under development that you're interested in and be a good beta-tester. There's a natural progression from helping test programs to helping debug them to helping modify them. You'll learn a lot this way, and generate good karma with people who will help you later on.

3. Publish Useful Information

Another good thing is to collect and filter useful and interesting information into web pages or documents like Frequently Asked Questions (FAQ) lists, and make those generally available.

Maintainers of major technical FAQs get almost as much respect as open-source authors.

4. Help Keep the Infrastructure Working

The hacker culture (and the engineering development of the Internet, for that matter) is run by volunteers. There's a lot of necessary but unglamorous work that needs done to keep it going—administering mailing lists, moderating newsgroups, maintaining large software archive sites, developing RFCs and other technical standards.

People who do this sort of thing well get a lot of respect, because everybody knows these jobs are huge time sinks and not as much fun as playing with code. Doing them shows dedication.

5. Serve the Hacker Culture Itself

Finally, you can serve and propagate the culture itself (by, for example, writing an accurate primer on how to become a hacker :-)). This is not something you'll be positioned to do until you've been around for while and become well-known for one of the first four things.

The hacker culture doesn't have leaders, exactly, but it does have culture heroes and tribal elders and historians and spokespeople. When you've been in the trenches long enough, you may grow into one of these. Beware: hackers distrust blatant ego in their tribal elders, so visibly reaching for this kind of fame is dangerous. Rather than striving for it, you have to sort of position yourself so it drops in your lap, and then be modest and gracious about your status.

The Hacker/Nerd Connection

Contrary to popular myth, you don't have to be a nerd to be a hacker. It does help, however, and many hackers are in fact nerds. Being a social outcast helps you stay concentrated on the really important things, like thinking and hacking.

For this reason, many hackers have adopted the label 'nerd' and even use the harsher term 'geek' as a badge of pride—it's a way of declaring their independence from normal social expectations. See The Geek Page (*http://samsara.circus.com/~omni/geek.html*) for extensive discussion.

If you can manage to concentrate enough on hacking to be good at it and still have a life, that's fine. This is a lot easier today than it was when I was a newbie in the 1970s; mainstream culture is much friendlier to techno-nerds now. There are even growing numbers of people who realize that hackers are often high-quality lover and spouse material.

If you're attracted to hacking because you don't have a life, that's okay too—at least you won't have trouble concentrating. Maybe you'll get a life later on.

Points for Style

Again, to be a hacker, you have to enter the hacker mindset. There are some things you can do when you're not at a computer that seem to help. They're not substitutes for hacking (nothing is) but many hackers do them, and feel that they connect in some basic way with the essence of hacking.

- Learn to write your native language well. Though it's a common stereotype that programmers can't write, a surprising number of hackers (including all the best ones I know of) are able writers.

- Read science fiction. Go to science fiction conventions (a good way to meet hackers and proto-hackers).

- Study Zen, and/or take up martial arts. (The mental discipline seems similar in important ways.)

- Develop an analytical ear for music. Learn to appreciate peculiar kinds of music. Learn to play some musical instrument well, or how to sing.

- Develop your appreciation of puns and wordplay.

The more of these things you already do, the more likely it is that you are natural hacker material. Why these things in particular is not completely clear, but they're connected with a mix of left- and right-brain skills that seems to be important (hackers need to be able to both reason logically and step outside the apparent logic of a problem at a moment's notice).

Finally, a few things *not* to do:

- Don't use a silly, grandiose user ID or screen name.
- Don't get in flame wars on Usenet (or anywhere else).
- Don't call yourself a 'cyberpunk', and don't waste your time on anybody who does.
- Don't post or email writing that's full of spelling errors and bad grammar.

The only reputation you'll make doing any of these things is as a twit. Hackers have long memories—it could take you years to live your early blunders down enough to be accepted.

The problem with screen names or handles deserves some amplification. Concealing your identity behind a handle is a juvenile and silly behavior characteristic of crackers, warez d00dz, and other lower life forms. Hackers don't do this; they're proud of what they do and want it associated with their *real* names. So if you have a handle, drop it. In the hacker culture it will only mark you as a loser.

OTHER RESOURCES

Peter Seebach maintains an excellent Hacker FAQ (*http://www.plethora.net/~seebs/faqs/hacker.html*) for managers who don't understand how to deal with hackers. I have also written *A Brief History of Hackerdom*, (*http://www.tuxedo.org/~esr/writings/hacker-history/hacker-history.html*). *The Cathedral and the Bazaar*, (*http://www.tuxedo.org/~esr/writings/cathedral-bazaar/index.html*) explains a lot about how the Linux and open-source cultures work. I have addressed this topic even more directly in its sequel *Homesteading the Noosphere*, *http://www.tuxedo.org/~esr/writings/homesteading/*.

Frequently Asked Questions

Will you teach me how to hack?

Since first publishing this essay, I've gotten several requests a week (often several a day) from people to "teach me all about hacking". Unfortunately, I don't have the time or energy to do this; my own hacking projects, and traveling as an open-source advocate, take up 110% of my time.

Even if I did, hacking is an attitude and skill you basically have to teach yourself. You'll find that while real hackers want to help you, they won't respect you if you beg to be spoon-fed everything they know.

Learn a few things first. Show that you're trying, that you're capable of learning on your own. Then go to the hackers you meet with specific questions.

How can I get started, then?

The best way for you to get started would probably be to go to a LUG (Linux user group) meeting. You can find such groups on the LDP General Linux Information Page, *http://MetaLab.unc.edu/LDP/intro.html*; there is probably one near you, possibly associated with a college or university. LUG members will probably give you a Linux if you ask, and will certainly help you install one and get started.

When do you have to start? Is it too late for me to learn?

Any age at which you are motivated to start is a good age. Most people seem to get interested between ages 15 and 20, but I know of exceptions in both directions.

How long will it take me to learn to hack?

That depends on how talented you are and how hard you work at it. Most people can acquire a respectable skill set in 18 months to 2 years, if they concentrate. Don't think it ends there, though; if you are a real hacker, you will spend the rest of your life learning and perfecting your craft.

Are Visual Basic or Delphi good languages to start with?

No, because they're not portable. There are no open-source implementations of these languages, so you'd be locked into only those platforms the vendor chooses to support. Accepting that kind of monopoly situation is not the hacker way.

Visual Basic is especially awful. The fact that it's a proprietary Microsoft language is enough to disqualify it, and like other Basics it's a poorly designed language that will teach you bad programming habits.

One of those bad habits is becoming dependent on a single vendor's libraries, widgets, and development tools. In general, any language that isn't supported under at least Linux or one of the BSDs, and/or at least three different vendors' operating systems, is a poor one to learn to hack in.

Would you help me to crack a system, or teach me how to crack?

No. Anyone who can still ask such a question after reading this FAQ is too stupid to be educable even if I had the time for tutoring. Any emailed requests of this kind that I get will be ignored or answered with extreme rudeness.

How can I get the password for someone else's account?

This is cracking. Go away, idiot.

I've been cracked. Will you help me fend off further attacks?

No. Every time I've been asked this question so far, it's been from somebody running Windows. It is not possible to effectively secure Windows systems against crack attacks; the code and architecture simply have too many flaws, and securing Windows is like trying to bail out a boat with a sieve. The only reliable prevention is to switch to Linux or some other operating system with real security.

I'm having problems with my Windows software. Will you help me?

Yes. Go to a DOS prompt and type "format c:". The problems you are experiencing will cease within a few minutes.

Where can I find some real hackers to talk with?

The best way is to find a Unix or Linux user's group local to you and go to their meetings (you can find links to several lists of user groups on the LDP site at Metalab, *http://metalab.unc.edu/LDP/*).

(I used to say here that you wouldn't find any real hackers on IRC, but I'm given to understand this is changing. Apparently some real hacker communities, attached to things like GIMP and Perl, have IRC channels now.)

Can you recommend useful books about hacking-related subjects?

I maintain a Linux Reading List HOWTO, *http://sunsite.unc.edu/LDP/HOWTO/Reading-List-HOWTO/index.html*, that you may find helpful. The Loginataka may also be interesting.

What language should I learn first?

HTML, if you don't already know it. There are a lot of glossy, hype-intensive *bad* HTML books out there, and distressingly few good ones. The one I like best is *HTML: The Definitive Guide* (*http://www.oreilly.com/catalog/html3/*).

But HTML is not a full programming language. When you're ready to start programming, I would recommend starting with Python, *http://www.python.org*. You will hear a lot of people recommending Perl, and Perl is still more popular than Python, but it's harder to learn and (in my opinion) less well designed. There are web resources for beginners using Python at *http://www.deja.com/getdoc.xp?AN=523189453*.

C is really important, but it's also much more difficult than either Python or Perl. Don't try to learn it first.

Windows users, do *not* settle for Visual Basic. It will teach you bad habits, and it's not portable off Windows. Avoid.

What kind of hardware do I need?

It used to be that personal computers were rather underpowered and memory-poor, enough so that they placed artificial limits on a hacker's learning process. This stopped being true some time ago; any machine from an Intel 486DX50 up is more than powerful enough for development work, X, and Internet communications, and the smallest disks you can buy today are plenty big enough.

The important thing in choosing a machine on which to learn is whether its hardware is Linux-compatible (or BSD-compatible, should you choose to go that route). Again, this will be true for most modern machines; the only sticky areas are modems and printers; some machines have Windows-specific hardware that won't work with Linux.

There's a FAQ on hardware compatibility; the latest version is here, *http://users.bart.nl/˜patrickr/hardware-howto/Hardware-HOWTO.html*.

Do I need to hate and bash Microsoft?

No, you don't. Not that Microsoft isn't loathsome, but there was a hacker culture long before Microsoft and there will still be one when Microsoft is history. Any energy you spend hating Microsoft would be better spent on loving your craft. Write good code—that will bash Microsoft quite sufficiently without polluting your karma.

But won't open-source software leave programmers unable to make a living?

This seems unlikely—so far, the open-source software industry seems to be creating jobs rather than taking them away. If having a program written is a net economic gain over not having it written, a programmer will get paid whether or not the program is going to be free after it's done. And, no matter how much "free" software gets written, there always seems to be more demand for new and customized applications. I've written more about this at the Open Source (*http://www.open-source.org*) pages.

How can I get started? Where can I get a free Unix?

Elsewhere on this page I include pointers to where to get the most commonly used free Unix. To be a hacker you need motivation and initiative and the ability to educate yourself. Start now . . . .

APPENDIX B

STATISTICAL TRENDS IN THE FETCHMAIL PROJECT'S GROWTH

❖ ❖ ❖

The scattergram below was made with Gnuplot 3.7 from data pulled directly out of the fetchmail project NEWS file using two custom shellscripts available on the project website.

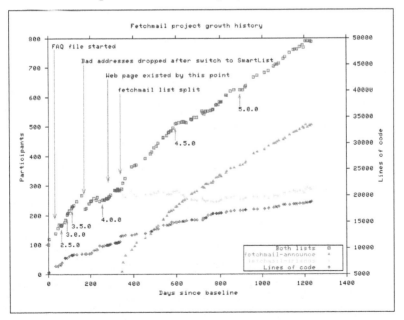

The graph shows the population growth of the fetchmail project. The horizontal scale is days since baseline, which is when I started collecting statistics in October 1996 at version 1.9.0. Left vertical scale is number of participants. There is one data point for each release; therefore, the changes in density of marks indicate release frequency.

The peak in the earliest part of the graph (before the note "Bad addresses dropped") seems to be an artifact; I was not regularly dropping addresses that became invalid at the time. Turnover on the list seems to be about 5% per month (but that's just my estimate, I don't have numbers on this).

The scatter of squares is total participants. The scatter of crosses is the count of people on fetchmail-friends after I split the list. The scatter of triangles is the population of fetchmail-announce after the split.

The scatter of diamonds tracks project size in lines of code (right vertical axis). The scale relationship between this scatter and the other three is arbitrary.

This graph is quite revealing. Several trends stand out:

- Over time, the project population displays rather consistent linear growth.

- The key event in the project's lifetime was release 4.3.0 in October 1997, when I declared the code to be out of development and in maintainance mode, and split the fetchmail list.

- The run-up to 4.3.0 saw the most intensive spate of releases in the project's history (the gap in that run happened when I took a two-week vacation). It was followed by a significant slowdown.

- After 4.3.0, the developer population remained fairly stable around an average of about 250 participants.

- Essentially all population growth after 4.3.0 happened on the announce list, among people using fetchmail but not active co-developers.

- The growth trend in code size looks sublinear, perhaps logarithmic.

The linear growth trend in population is particularly interesting; a priori we might expect geometric or logistic growth, given that the project spreads by word of mouth.

It has been suggested that the linear growth rate is the result of a situation in which both number of projects and the population of eligible programmers are rising on trend curves of the same (probably exponential) rate.

There are some web pages doing similar things:

- *http://kitenet.net/programs/debhelper/stats/* contains growth statistics on the debhelper packaging utility.

- *http://durak.org:81/sean/pubs/kfc/* is a page on the vocabulary of the Linux kernel.

NOTES, BIBLIOGRAPHY, AND ACKNOWLEDGMENTS

✦ ✦ ✦

A BRIEF HISTORY OF HACKERDOM

NOTES

1. David E. Lundstrom. "Real Programmer." In *A Few Good Men From UNIVAC*, 1987. An anecdotal history.

2. Levy, Steven. *Hackers*. Garden City, N.Y.: Anchor/Doubleday, 1984.

3. Raymond, Eric S. *The New Hacker's Dictionary*. Cambridge: MIT Press, 1996.

————

THE CATHEDRAL AND THE BAZAAR

NOTES

1. In *Programing Pearls*, the noted computer-science aphorist Jon Bentley comments on Brooks's observation with "If you plan to throw one away, you will throw away two." He is almost certainly right. The point of Brooks's observation, and Bentley's, isn't merely that you should expect the first attempt to be wrong, it's that starting over with the right idea is usually more effective than trying to salvage a mess.

2. Examples of successful open-source, bazaar development predating the Internet explosion and unrelated to the Unix and Internet traditions have existed. The development of the info-Zip (*http://www.cdrom.com/pub/infozip/*)

compression utility during 1990–1992, primarily for DOS machines, was one such example. Another was the RBBS bulletin board system (again for DOS), which began in 1983 and developed a sufficiently strong community that there have been fairly regular releases up to the present (mid-1999) despite the huge technical advantages of Internet mail and file-sharing over local BBSs. While the info-Zip community relied to some extent on Internet mail, the RBBS developer culture was actually able to base a substantial online community on RBBS that was completely independent of the TCP/IP infrastructure.

3. That transparency and peer review are valuable for taming the complexity of OS development turns out, after all, not to be a new concept. In 1965, very early in the history of time-sharing operating systems, Corbató and Vyssotsky, co-designers of the Multics operating system (*http://www.multicians.org/fjcc1.html*) wrote:

> It is expected that the Multics system will be published when it is operating substantially.... Such publication is desirable for two reasons: First, the system should withstand public scrutiny and criticism volunteered by interested readers; second, in an age of increasing complexity, it is an obligation to present and future system designers to make the inner operating system as lucid as possible so as to reveal the basic system issues.

4. John Hasler has suggested an interesting explanation for the fact that duplication of effort doesn't seem to be a net drag on open-source development. He proposes what I'll dub "Hasler's Law": the costs of duplicated work tend to scale sub-quadratically with team size—that is, more slowly than the planning and management overhead that would be needed to eliminate them.

This claim actually does not contradict Brooks's Law. It may be the case that total complexity overhead and vulnerability to bugs scales with the square of team size, but that the costs from *duplicated* work are nevertheless a special case that scales more slowly. It's not hard to develop plausible reasons for this, starting with the undoubted fact that it is much easier to agree on functional boundaries between different developers' code that will prevent duplication of effort than it is to prevent the kinds of unplanned bad interactions across the whole system that underly most bugs.

The combination of Linus's Law and Hasler's Law suggests that there are actually three critical size regimes in software projects. On small projects (I would say one to at most three developers) no management structure more elaborate than picking a lead programmer is needed. And there is some intermediate range above that in which the cost of traditional management is relatively low, so its benefits from avoiding duplication of effort, bug-tracking, and pushing to see that details are not overlooked actually net out positive.

Above that, however, the combination of Linus's Law and Hasler's Law suggests there is a large-project range in which the costs and problems of traditional management rise much faster than the expected cost from duplication of effort. Not the least of these costs is a structural inability to harness the many-eyeballs effect, which (as we've seen) seems to do a much better job than traditional management at making sure bugs and details are not overlooked. Thus, in the large-project case, the combination of these laws effectively drives the net payoff of traditional management to zero.

5. The split between Linux's experimental and stable versions has another function related to, but distinct from, hedging risk. The split attacks another problem: the deadliness of deadlines. When programmers are held both to an immutable feature list and a fixed drop-dead date, quality goes out the window and there is likely a colossal mess in the making. I am indebted to Marco Iansiti and Alan MacCormack of the Harvard Business School for showing me me evidence that relaxing either one of these constraints can make scheduling workable.

One way to do this is to fix the deadline but leave the feature list flexible, allowing features to drop off if not completed by deadline. This is essentially the strategy of the "stable" kernel branch; Alan Cox (the stable-kernel maintainer) puts out releases at fairly regular intervals, but makes no guarantees about when particular bugs will be fixed or what features will be back-ported from the experimental branch.

The other way to do this is to set a desired feature list and deliver only when it is done. This is essentially the strategy of the "experimental" kernel branch. De Marco and Lister cited research showing that this scheduling policy ("wake me up when it's done") produces not only the highest quality but, on average, shorter delivery times than either "realistic" or "aggressive" scheduling.

I have come to suspect (as of early 2000) that in earlier versions of this essay I severely underestimated the importance of the "wake me up when it's done" anti-deadline policy to the open-source community's productivity and quality. General experience with the rushed GNOME 1.0 release in 1999 suggests that pressure for a premature release can neutralize many of the quality benefits open source normally confers.

It may well turn out to be that the process transparency of open source is one of three co-equal drivers of its quality, along with "wake me up when it's done" scheduling and developer self-selection.

6. It's tempting, and not entirely inaccurate, to see the core-plus-halo organization characteristic of open-source projects as an Internet-enabled spin on Brooks's own recommendation for solving the N-squared complexity problem, the "surgical-team" organization—but the differences are significant. The constellation of specialist roles such as "code librarian" that Brooks envisioned around the team leader doesn't really exist; those roles are executed instead by generalists aided by toolsets quite a bit more powerful than those of Brooks's day. Also, the open-source culture leans heavily on strong Unix traditions of modularity, APIs, and information hiding—none of which were elements of Brooks's prescription.

7. The respondent who pointed out to me the effect of widely varying trace path lengths on the difficulty of characterizing a bug speculated that trace-path difficulty for multiple symptoms of the same bug varies "exponentially" (which I take to mean on a Gaussian or Poisson distribution, and agree seems very plausible). If it is experimentally possible to get a handle on the shape of this distribution, that would be extremely valuable data. Large departures from a

flat equal-probability distribution of trace difficulty would suggest that even solo developers should emulate the bazaar strategy by bounding the time they spend on tracing a given symptom before they switch to another. Persistence may not always be a virtue . . . .

8.   An issue related to whether one can start projects from zero in the bazaar style is whether the bazaar style is capable of supporting truly innovative work. Some claim that, lacking strong leadership, the bazaar can only handle the cloning and improvement of ideas already present at the engineering state-of-the-art, but is unable to push the state-of-the-art. This argument was perhaps most infamously made by the Halloween Documents, *http://www.opensource.org/halloween/*, two embarrassing internal Microsoft memoranda written about the open-source phenomenon. The authors compared Linux's development of a Unix-like operating system to "chasing tail-lights", and opined "(once a project has achieved 'parity' with the state-of-the-art), the level of management necessary to push towards new frontiers becomes massive".

There are serious errors of fact implied in this argument. One is exposed when the Halloween authors themseselves later observe that "Often [. . .] new research ideas are first implemented and available on Linux before they are available/incorporated into other platforms."

If we read "open source" for "Linux", we see that this is far from a new phenomenon. Historically, the open-source community did not invent Emacs or the World Wide Web or the Internet itself by chasing taillights or being massively managed—and in the present, there is so much innovative work going on in open source that one is spoiled for choice. The GNOME project (to pick one of many) is pushing the state of the art in GUIs and object technology hard enough to have attracted considerable notice in the computer trade press well outside the Linux community. Other examples are legion, as a visit to Freshmeat (*http://freshmeat.net/*) on any given day will quickly prove.

But there is a more fundamental error in the implicit assumption that the *cathedral model* (or the bazaar model, or any other kind of management structure) can somehow make innovation happen reliably. This is nonsense. Gangs don't have breakthrough insights—even volunteer groups of bazaar anarchists are usually incapable of genuine originality, let alone corporate committees of people with a survival stake in some status quo ante. *Insight comes from individuals.* The most their surrounding social machinery can ever hope to do is to be *responsive* to breakthrough insights—to nourish and reward and rigorously test them instead of squashing them.

Some will characterize this as a romantic view, a reversion to outmoded lone-inventor stereotypes. Not so; I am not asserting that groups are incapable of *developing* breakthrough insights once they have been hatched; indeed, we learn from the peer-review process that such development groups are essential to producing a high-quality result. Rather I am pointing out that every such group development starts from—is necessarily sparked by—one good idea in one person's head. Cathedrals and bazaars and other social structures can catch that lightning and refine it, but they cannot make it on demand.

Therefore the root problem of innovation (in software, or anywhere else) is indeed how not to squash it—but, even more fundamentally, it is *how to grow lots of people who can have insights in the first place.*

To suppose that cathedral-style development could manage this trick but the low entry barriers and process fluidity of the bazaar cannot would be absurd. If what it takes is one person with one good idea, then a social milieu in which one person can rapidly attract the cooperation of hundreds or thousands of others with that good idea is going inevitably to out-innovate any in which the person has to do a political sales job to a hierarchy before he can work on his idea without risk of getting fired.

And, indeed, if we look at the history of software innovation by organizations using the cathedral model, we quickly find it is rather rare. Large corporations rely on university research for new ideas (thus the Halloween Documents authors' unease about Linux's facility at coopting that research more rapidly). Or they buy out small companies built around some innovator's brain. In neither case is the innovation native to the cathedral culture; indeed, many innovations so imported end up being quietly suffocated under the "massive level of management" the Halloween Documents' authors so extol.

That, however, is a negative point. The reader would be better served by a positive one. I suggest the following:

- Pick a criterion for originality that you believe you can apply consistently. If your definition is "I know it when I see it", that's not a problem for purposes of this test.

- Pick any closed-source operating system competing with Linux, and a best source for accounts of current development work on it.

- Watch that source and Freshmeat for one month. Every day, count the number of release announcements on Freshmeat that you consider 'original' work. Apply the same definition of 'original' to announcements for that other OS and count them.

- Thirty days later, total up both figures.

The day I wrote this, Freshmeat carried 22 release announcements, of which 3 appear they might push state-of-the-art in some respect, This was a slow day for Freshmeat, but I will be astonished if any reader reports as many as 3 likely innovations *a month* in any closed-source channel.

9. We now have history on a project that, in several ways, may provide a more indicative test of the bazaar premise than fetchmail; EGCS, *http://egcs.cygnus.com/*, the Experimental GNU Compiler System.

This project was announced in mid-August of 1997 as a conscious attempt to apply the ideas in the early public versions of *The Cathedral and the Bazaar.* The project founders felt that the development of GCC, the Gnu C Compiler, had been stagnating. For about 20 months afterwards, GCC and EGCS continued as parallel products—both drawing from the same Internet developer population, both starting from the same GCC source base, both using pretty much the same Unix toolsets and development environment. The projects differed only in that EGCS consciously tried to apply the bazaar tactics I have previously described, while GCC retained a more cathedral-like organization with a closed developer group and infrequent releases.

This was about as close to a controlled experiment as one could ask for, and the results were dramatic. Within months, the EGCS versions had pulled substantially ahead in features; better optimization, better support for FORTRAN and C++. Many people found the EGCS development snapshots to be more reliable than the most recent stable version of GCC, and major Linux distributions began to switch to EGCS.

In April of 1999, the Free Software Foundation (the official sponsors of GCC) dissolved the original GCC development group and officially handed control of the project to the the EGCS steering team.

10. Of course, Kropotkin's critique and Linus's Law raise some wider issues about the cybernetics of social organizations. Another folk theorem of software engineering suggests one of them; Conway's Law—commonly stated as "If you have four groups working on a compiler, you'll get a 4-pass compiler." The original statement was more general: "Organizations which design systems are constrained to produce designs which are copies of the communication structures of these organizations." We might put it more succinctly as "The means determine the ends", or even "Process becomes product".

It is accordingly worth noting that in the open-source community organizational form and function match on many levels. The network is everything and everywhere: not just the Internet, but the people doing the work form a distributed, loosely coupled, peer-to-peer network that provides multiple redundancy and degrades very gracefully. In both networks, each node is important only to the extent that other nodes want to cooperate with it.

The peer-to-peer part is essential to the community's astonishing productivity. The point Kropotkin was trying to make about power relationships is developed further by the 'SNAFU Principle': "True communication is possible only between equals, because inferiors are more consistently rewarded for telling their superiors pleasant lies than for telling the truth." Creative teamwork utterly depends on true communication and is thus very seriously hindered by the presence of power relationships. The open-source community, effectively free of such power relationships, is teaching us by contrast how dreadfully much they cost in bugs, in lowered productivity, and in lost opportunities.

Further, the SNAFU principle predicts in authoritarian organizations a progressive disconnect between decision-makers and reality, as more and more of the input to those who decide tends to become pleasant lies. The way this plays out in conventional software development is easy to see; there are strong incentives for the inferiors to hide, ignore, and minimize problems. When this process becomes product, software is a disaster.

Bibliography

I quoted several bits from Frederick P. Brooks's classic *The Mythical Man-Month* because, in many respects, his insights have yet to be improved upon. I heartily recommend the 25th Anniversary edition from Addison-Wesley, which adds his "No Silver Bullet" paper (1986).

The new edition is wrapped up by an invaluable 20-years-later retrospective in which Brooks forthrightly admits to the few judgements in the original text that have not stood the test of time. I first read the retrospective after the first public version of this essay was substantially complete, and was surprised to discover that Brooks attributed bazaar-like practices to Microsoft! (In fact, however, this attribution turned out to be mistaken. In 1998 we learned from the Halloween Documents (*http://www.opensource.org/halloween/*) that Microsoft's internal developer community is heavily balkanized, with the kind of general source access needed to support a bazaar not even truly possible.)

Gerald M. Weinberg's *The Psychology Of Computer Programming* (New York: Van Nostrand Reinhold, 1971) introduced the rather unfortunately-labeled concept of "egoless programming". While he was nowhere near the first person to realize the futility of the "principle of command", he was probably the first to recognize and argue the point in particular connection with software development.

Richard P. Gabriel, contemplating the Unix culture of the pre-Linux era, reluctantly argued for the superiority of a primitive bazaar-like model in his 1989 paper "LISP: Good News, Bad News, and How to Win Big". Though dated in some respects, this essay is still rightly celebrated among LISP fans (including me). A correspondent reminded me that the section titled "Worse Is Better" reads almost as an anticipation of Linux. The paper is accessible on the World Wide Web at *http://www.naggum.no/worse-is-better.html*".

De Marco's and Lister's *Peopleware: Productive Projects and Teams* (New York: Dorset House, 1987) is an underappreciated gem that I was delighted to see Fred Brooks cite in his retrospective. While little of what the authors have to say is directly applicable to the Linux or open-source communities, the authors' insight into the conditions necessary for creative work is acute and worthwhile for anyone attempting to import some of the bazaar model's virtues into a commercial context.

Finally, I must admit that I very nearly called this essay "The Cathedral and the Agora", the latter term being the Greek for an open market or public meeting place. The seminal "agoric systems" papers by Mark Miller and Eric Drexler, by describing the emergent properties of market-like computational ecologies, helped prepare me to think clearly about analogous phenomena in the open-source culture when Linux rubbed my nose in them five years later. These papers are available on the Web at *http://www.agorics.com/agorpapers.html*".

ACKNOWLEDGMENTS

This essay was improved by conversations with a large number of people who helped debug it. Particular thanks to Jeff Dutky (*dutky@wam.umd.edu*), who suggested the "debugging is parallelizable" formulation, and helped develop the analysis that proceeds from it. Also to Nancy Lebovitz (*nancyl@universe.digex.net*) for her suggestion that I emulate Weinberg by quoting Kropotkin. Perceptive criticisms also came from Joan Eslinger (*wombat@kilimanjaro.engr.sgi.com*) and Marty Franz (*marty@net-link.net*) of the General Technics list. Glen Vandenburg (*glv@vanderburg.org*) pointed out the importance of self-selection in contributor populations and suggested the fruitful idea that much development rectifies 'bugs of omission'; Daniel Upper (*upper@peak.org*) suggested the natural analogies for this. I'm grateful to the members of PLUG, the Philadelphia Linux User's Group, for providing the first test audience for the first public version of this essay. Paula Matuszek (*matusp00@mh.us.sbphrd.com*) enlightened me about the practice of software management. Phil Hudson (*phil.hudson@iname.com*) reminded me that the social organization of the hacker culture mirrors the organization of its software, and vice-versa. John Buck (*johnbuck@sea.ece.umassd.edu*) pointed out that MATLAB makes an instructive parallel to Emacs. Russell Johnston (*russjj@mail.com*) brought me to consciousness about some of the mechanisms discussed in "How Many Eyeballs Tame Complexity". Finally, Linus Torvalds's comments were helpful and his early endorsement very encouraging.

HOMESTEADING THE NOOSPHERE

NOTES

1. The term 'noosphere' is an obscure term of art in philosophy. It is pronounced KNOW-uh-sfeer (two o-sounds, one long and stressed, one short and unstressed tending towards schwa). If one is being excruciatingly correct about one's orthography, the term is properly spelled with a diaeresis over the second 'o' to mark it as a separate vowel.

   In more detail; this term for "the sphere of human thought" derives from the Greek 'noos' meaning 'mind', 'intelligence,' or 'breath'. It was invented by E. LeRoy in *Les origines humaines et l'evolution de l'intelligence* (Paris, 1928). It was popularized first by the Russian biologist and pioneering ecologist Vladimir Ivanovich Vernadsky, (1863–1945), then by the Jesuit paleontologist/philosopher Pierre Teilhard de Chardin (1881–1955). It is with Teilhard de Chardin's theory of future evolution to a form of pure mind culminating in union with the Godhead that the term is now primarily associated.

2. David Friedman, one of the most lucid and accessible thinkers in contemporary economics, has written an excellent outline of the history and logic of intellectual-property law (*http://www.best.com/~ddfr/Academic/Course_Pages /L_and_E_LS_98/Why_Is_Law/Why_Is_Law_Chapter_11.html*). I recommend it as a starting point to anyone interested in these issues.

3. One interesting difference between the Linux and BSD worlds is that the Linux kernel (and associated OS core utilities) have never forked, but BSD's has, at least three times. What makes this interesting is that the social structure of the BSD groups is centralized in a way intended to define clear lines of authority and to prevent forking, while the decentralized and amorphous Linux community takes no such measures. It appears that the projects that open up development the most actually have the *least* tendency to fork!

   Henry Spencer (*henry@spsystems.net*) suggests that, in general, the stability of a political system is inversely proportional to the height of the entry barriers to its political process. His analysis is worth quoting here:

   > *One major strength of a relatively open democracy is that most potential revolutionaries find it easier to make progress toward their objectives by working via the system rather by attacking it. This strength is easily undermined if established parties act together to 'raise the bar', making it more difficult for small dissatisfied groups to see some progress made toward their goals.*

   > *(A similar principle can be found in economics. Open markets have the strongest competition, and generally the best and cheapest products. Because of this, it's very much in the best interests of established companies to make market entry more difficult — for example, by convincing governments to require elaborate RFI testing on computers, or by creating 'consensus' standards that are so complex that they cannot be implemented effectively from scratch*

without large resources. The markets with the strongest entry barriers are the ones that come under the strongest attack from revolutionaries, e.g., the Internet and the Justice Dept. vs. the Bell System.)

An open process with low entry barriers encourages participation rather than secession, because one can get results without the high overheads of secession. The results may not be as impressive as what could be achieved by seceding, but they come at a lower price, and most people will consider that an acceptable tradeoff. (When the Spanish government revoked Franco's anti-Basque laws and offered the Basque provinces their own schools and limited local autonomy, most of the Basque Separatist movement evaporated almost overnight. Only the hard-core Marxists insisted that it wasn't good enough.)

4. There are some subtleties about rogue patches. One can divide them into 'friendly' and 'unfriendly' types. A 'friendly' patch is designed to be merged back into the project's main-line sources under the maintainer's control (whether or not that merge actually happens); an 'unfriendly' one is intended to yank the project in a direction the maintainer doesn't approve. Some projects (notably the Linux kernel itself) are pretty relaxed about friendly patches and even encourage independent distribution of them as part of their beta-test phase. An unfriendly patch, on the other hand, represents a decision to compete with the original and is a serious matter. Maintaining a whole raft of unfriendly patches tends to lead to forking.

5. I am indebted to Michael Funk (*mwfunk@uncc.campus.mci.net*) for pointing out how instructive a contrast with hackers the pirate culture is. Linus Walleij has posted an analysis of their cultural dynamics that differs from mine (describing them as a scarcity culture) in *A Comment on 'Warez D00dz' Culture* (*http://www.df.lth.se/˜triad/papers/Raymond_D00dz.html"*).

    The contrast may not last. Former cracker Andrej Brandt (*andy@pilgrim.cs.net.pl*) reports that he believes the cracker/warez d00dz culture is now withering away, with its brightest people and leaders assimilating to the open-source world. Independent evidence for this view may be provided by a precedent-breaking July 1999 action of the cracker group calling itself "Cult of the Dead Cow". They have released their "Back Orifice 2000" for breaking Microsoft Windows security tools under the GPL.

6. In evolutionary terms, the craftsman's urge itself may (like internalized ethics) be a result of the high risk and cost of deception. Evolutionary psychologists have collected experimental evidence [1] that human beings have brain logic specialized for detecting social deceptions, and it is fairly easy to see why our ancestors should have been selected for ability to detect cheating. Therefore, if one wishes to have a reputation for personality traits that confer advantage but are risky or costly, it may actually be better tactics to actually have these traits than to fake them. ("Honesty is the best policy.")

    Evolutionary psychologists have suggested that this explains behavior like barroom fights. Among younger adult male humans, having a reputation for toughness is both socially and (even in today's feminist-influenced climate) sexually useful. Faking toughness, however, is extremely risky; the negative result of being found out leaves one in a worse position than never having claimed the trait. The cost of deception is so high that it is sometimes better minimaxing to internalize toughness and risk serious injury in a fight to prove it. Parallel observations have been made about less controversial traits like honesty.

Though the primary meditation-like rewards of creative work should not be underestimated, the craftsman's urge is probably at least in part just such an internalization (where the base trait is 'capacity for painstaking work' or something similar).

Handicap theory may also be relevant. The peacock's gaudy tail and the stag's massive rack of antlers are sexy to females because they send a message about the health of the male (and, consequently, its fitness to sire healthy offspring). They say: "I am so vigorous that I can afford to waste a lot of energy on this extravagant display." Giving away source code, like owning a sports car, is very similar to such showy, wasteful finery—it's expense without obvious return, and makes the giver at least theoretically very sexy.

7. A concise summary of Maslow's hierarchy and related theories is available on the Web at *http://www.valdosta.peachnet.edu/˜whuitt/psy702/regsys/ maslow.html "*.

8. However, demanding humility from leaders may be a more general character-istic of gift or abundance cultures. David Christie (*dc@netscape.com*) reports on a trip through the outer islands of Fiji:

     In Fijian village chiefs, we observed the same sort of self-deprecat-ing, low-key leadership style that you attribute to open source pro-ject leaders. [. . .] Though accorded great respect and of course all of whatever actual power there is in Fiji, the chiefs we met demon-strated genuine humility and often a saint-like acceptance of their duty. This is particularly interesting given that being chief is a hereditary role, not an elected position or a popularity contest. Somehow they are trained to it by the culture itself, although they are born to it, not chosen by their peers." He goes on to emphasize that he believes the characteristic style of Fijian chiefs springs from the difficulty of compelling cooperation: a chief has "no big carrot or big stick".

9. As a matter of observable fact, people who found successful projects gather more prestige than people who do arguably equal amounts of work debug-ging and assisting with successful projects. An earlier version of this essay asked "Is this a rational valuation of comparative effort, or is it a second-order effect of the unconscious territorial model we have adduced here?" Sev-eral respondents suggested persuasive and essentially equivalent theories. The following analysis by Ryan Waldron (*rew@erebor.com*) puts the case well:

     In the context of the Lockean land theory, one who establishes a new and successful project has essentially discovered or opened up new territory on which others can homestead. For most successful projects, there is a pattern of declining returns, so that after a while, the credit for contributions to a project has become so

> *diffuse that it is hard for significant reputation to accrete to a late*
> *participant, regardless of the quality of his work.*
>
> *For instance, how good a job would I have to do making modifica-*
> *tions to the Perl code to have even a fraction of the recognition for*
> *my participation that Larry, Tom, Randall, and others have*
> *achieved?*
>
> *However, if a new project is founded [by someone else] tomorrow,*
> *and I am an early and frequent participant in it, my ability to share*
> *in the respect generated by such a successful project is greatly*
> *enhanced by my early participation therein (assuming similar qual-*
> *ity of contributions). I reckon it to be similar to those who invest*
> *in Microsoft stock early and those who invest in it later. Everyone*
> *may profit, but early participants profit more. Therefore, at some*
> *point I will be more interested in a new and successful IPO than I*
> *will be in participating in the continual increase of an existing body*
> *of corporate stock.*

Ryan Waldron's analogy can be extended. The project founder has to do a missionary sell of a new idea that may or may not be acceptable or of use to others. Thus the founder incurs something analogous to an IPO risk (of possible damage to their reputation), more so than others who assist with a project that has already garnered some acceptance by their peers. The founder's reward is consistent despite the fact that the assistants may be putting in more work in real terms. This is easily seen as analogous to the relationship between risk and rewards in an exchange economy.

Other respondents have observed that our nervous system is tuned to perceive differences, not steady state. The revolutionary change evidenced by the creation of a new project is therefore much more noticeable than the cumulative effect of constant incremental improvement. Thus Linus is revered as the father of Linux, although the net effect of improvements by thousands of other contributors have done more to contribute to the success of the OS than one man's work ever could.

10. The phrase "de-commoditizing" is a reference to the Halloween Documents (*http://www.opensource.org/halloween/*) in which Microsoft used "de-commoditize" quite frankly to refer to their most effective long-term strategy for maintaining an exploitative monopoly lock on customers.

11. A respondent points out that the values surrounding the "You're not a hacker until other hackers call you a hacker" norm parallel ideals professed (if not always achieved) by other meritocratic brotherhoods within social elites sufficiently wealthy to escape the surrounding scarcity economy. In the medieval European ideal of knighthood, for example, the aspiring knight was expected to fight for the right, to seek honor rather than gain, to take the side of the weak and oppressed, and to constantly seek challenges that tested his prowess to the utmost. In return, the knight-aspirant could regard himself (and be regarded by others) as among the best of the best—but only after his skill and virtue had been admitted and ratified by other knights. In the knightly ideal extolled by the Arthurian tales and Chansons de Geste we see a mix of idealism, continual self-challenge, and status-seeking similar to that which

animates hackers today. It seems likely that similar values and behavioral norms should evolve around any skill that both requires great dedication and confers a kind of power.

12. The Free Software Foundation's main website (*http://www.gnu.org/philoso-phy/motivation.html*") carries an article that summarizes the results of many of these studies. The quotes in this essay are excerpted from there.

Bibliography

Miller, William Ian. *Bloodtaking and Peacemaking: Feud, Law, and Society in Saga Iceland*. Chicago: University of Chicago Press, 1990. A fascinating study of Icelandic folkmoot law, which both illuminates the ancestry of the Lockean theory of property and describes the later stages of a historical process by which custom passed into customary law and thence to written law.

Malaclypse the Younger. *Principia Discordia, or How I Found Goddess and What I Did To Her When I Found Her*. Loompanics, 1980. There is much enlightening silliness to be found in Discordianism. Amidst it, the 'SNAFU principle' provides a rather trenchant analysis of why command hierarchies don't scale well. There's a browseable HTML version, *http://www.cs.cmu.edu/~tilt/principia/*.

Barkow, J.L. Cosmides, and J. Tooby (Eds.). *The Adapted Mind: Evolutionary Psychology and the Generation of Culture*. New York: Oxford University Press, 1992. An excellent introduction to evolutionary psychology. Some of the papers bear directly on the three cultural types I discuss (command/exchange/gift), suggesting that these patterns are wired into the human psyche fairly deep.

Goldhaber, Michael K.: "The Attention Economy and the Net", *http://www.firstmonday.dk/issues/issue2_4/goldhaber*". I discovered this paper after my version 1.7. It has obvious flaws (Goldhaber's argument for the inapplicability of economic reasoning to attention does not bear close examination), but Goldhaber nevertheless has funny and perceptive things to say about the role of attention-seeking in organizing behavior. The prestige or peer repute I have discussed can fruitfully be viewed as a particular case of attention in his sense.

I have summarized the history of the hacker culture in *A Brief History of Hackerdom*, *http://www.tuxedo.org/~esr/faqs/hacker-hist.html*". The book that will explain it really well remains to be written, probably not by me.

ACKNOWLEDGMENTS

Robert Lanphier (*robla@real.com*) contributed much to the discussion of egoless behavior. Eric Kidd (*eric.kidd@pobox.com*) highlighted the role of valuing humility in preventing cults of personality. The section on global effects was inspired by comments from Daniel Burn (*daniel@tsathog-gua.lab.usyd.edu.au*). Mike Whitaker (*mrw@entropic.co.uk*) inspired the main thread in the section on acculturation. Chris Phoenix (*cphoenix@best.com*) pointed out the importance of the fact that hackers cannot gain reputation by doing other hackers down. A.J. Venter (*JAVenter@africon.co.za*) pointed out parallels with the medieval ideal of knighthood. Ian Lance Taylor (*ian@airs.com*) sent careful criticisms of the reputation-game model, which motivated me to think through and explain my assumptions more clearly.

THE MAGIC CAULDRON

NOTES

1. The underprovision problem would in fact scale linearly with a number of users if we assumed programming talent to be uniformly distributed in the project user population as it expands over time. This is not, however, the case.

    The incentives discussed in 2 (and some more conventionally economic ones as well) imply that qualified people tend to seek projects that match their interests, as well as the projects seeking them. Accordingly, theory suggests (and experience tends to confirm) that the most valuable (most qualified and motivated) people tend to discover the projects for which they fit well relatively early in the projects' life cycles, with a corresponding fall-off later on.

    Hard data are lacking, but on the basis of experience I strongly suspect the assimilation of talent over a growing project's lifetime tends to follow a classical logistic curve.

2. Shawn Hargreaves has written a good analysis of the applicability of open-source methods to games in *Playing the Open Source Game* (*http://www.talula.demon.co.uk/games.html*").

3. Note for accountants: the argument that service costs will eventually swamp a fixed up-front price still works if we move from constant dollars to discounted present value, because future sale revenue discounts in parallel with future service costs.

    A similar but more sophisticated counter to the argument is to observe that, per-copy, service cost will go to zero when the buyer stops using the software; therefore you can still win, if the user stops before he/she has generated too much service cost. This is basically just another form of the argument that factory pricing rewards the production of shelfware. Perhaps a more instructive way to put it would be that the risk that your service costs will swamp the purchase revenue rises with the expected period of usefulness of the software. Thus, the factory model penalizes quality.

4. Wayne Gramlich (*Wayne@Gramlich.Net*) has proposed that the persistance of the factory model is partly due to antiquated accounting rules, formulated when machines and buildings were more important and people less so. Software company books show the computers, office furniture, and buildings as assets and the programmers are expenses. Of course, in reality, the programmers are the true assets and the computers, office equipment, and buildings hardly matter at all. This perverse valuation is sustained by IRS and stock-market pressure for stable and uniform accounting rules that reduce the complexity of assigning a dollar figure to the company's value. The resulting drag has prevented the rules from keeping up with reality.

On this view, pinning a high price to the bits in the product (independent of future service value) is partly a sort of defense mechanism, a way of agreeing for all parties involved to pretend that the ontological ground hasn't fallen out from under the standard accounting rules.

(Gramlich also points out that these rules underpin the bizarre and often self-destructive acquisition sprees that many software companies tear off on after IPO: "Usually the software company issues some additional stock to build up a war chest. But they can't spend any of this money to beef up their programming staff, because the accounting rules would show that as increased expenses. Instead, the newly public software company has to grow by acquiring other software companies, because the accounting rules let you treat the acquisition as an investment.")

5. For a paradigmatic example of forking following defection, consult the history of OpenSSH. This project was belatedly forked from an early version of SSH (Secure Shell) after the latter went to a closed license.

BIBLIOGRAPHY

The Cathedral and the Bazaar, *http://www.tuxedo.org/~esr/writings/cathedral-bazaar/*

Homesteading the Noosphere, *http://www.tuxedo.org/~esr/writings/homesteading/*

De Marco and Lister. *Peopleware: Productive Projects and Teams.* New York: Dorset House, 1987.

Acknowledgments

Several stimulating discussions with David D. Friedman helped me refine the 'inverse commons' model of open-source cooperation. I am also indebted to Marshall van Alstyne for pointing out the conceptual importance of rivalrous information goods. Ray Ontko of the Indiana Group supplied helpful criticism. A good many people in audiences before whom I gave talks in the year leading up to June 1999 also helped; if you're one of those, you know who you are.

It's yet another testimony to the open-source model that this essay was substantially improved by email feedback I received within days after initial release. Lloyd Wood pointed out the importance of open-source software being 'future-proof'. and Doug Dante reminded me of the 'Free the Future' business model. A question from Adam Moorhouse led to the discussion of exclusion payoffs. Lionel Oliviera Gresse gave me a better name for one of the business models. Stephen Turnbull slapped me silly about careless handling of free-rider effects. Anthony Bailey and Warren Young corrected some facts in the Doom case study. Eric W. Sink contributed the insight that the factory model rewards shelfware.

For Further Reading

The beginnings of an academic analytical literature on open source have begun to appear. Related material on the Web can be found at the author's web page (*http://www.tuxedo.org/~esr/writings/cathedral-bazaar*).

Ross Anderson. *How to Cheat at the Lottery (or, Massively Parallel Requirements Engineering).* In this insightful, lucid and entertaining paper, the author presents the results of an experiment in applying bazaar-style parallelism not to coding but to the requirements analysis and system design for a difficult problem in computer security.

Available as *http://www.cl.cam.ac.uk/~rja14/lottery/lottery.html.*

Davis Baird. "Scientific Instrument Making, Epistemology, and the Conflict between Gift and Commodity Economies." In *Journal of the Society for Philosophy & Technology*, Volume 2, no. 3–4. This paper is interesting because, although it never refers to software or open source and is founded in earlier anthropological literature on gift cultures, it suggests an analysis similar in many respects to that in *Homesteading the Noosphere*.

Available on the Web at *http://scholar.lib.vt.edu/ejournals/SPT/ v2_n3n4html/baird.html*.

Asif Khalak, *Evolutionary Model for Open Source Software: Economic Impact*. The author attempts to model open-source market penetration analytically and to use computer simulation to examine the mosel's dependence on various cost and behavioral parameters. Presented at Genetic and Evolutionary Computation Conference, Ph.D. Workshop, July 1999.

Available as *http://web.mit.edu/asif/www/ace.html*.

Bojidar Mantarow. *Open Source Software as a New Business Model*. The author treats Red Hat Software as a case study in the effects of lowering barriers to entry in a mature market. This dissertation was submitted in partial fulfillment of the degree of MSc in International Management at University of Reading, August 1999.

Available as *http://www.lochnet.net/bozweb/academic/dissert.htm*.

Eben Moglen. "Anarchism Triumphant: Free Software and the Death of Copyright." This paper (originally published in the Columbia Law Review) contains a regrettably large number of errors in facts and logic, and the analytical content is very nearly smothered under misguided political polemic. Nevertheless, it is an entertaining and provocative read, worth plowing through if only for the context of Moglen's unforgettable corollary to Faraday's Law: "Wrap the Internet around every brain on the planet and spin the planet. Software flows in the wires."

Available as *http://old.law.columbia.edu/my_pubs/anarchism.html*.

———

INDEX

✦ ✦ ✦

Internet
  Free Software Foundation
    (FSF) and, 69
  Linux developers and, 21, 29
  popular discovery of, 17
  Unix development and, 51
Internet Explorer (Microsoft),
  135, 172
ITS (Incompatible Time-sharing
  System), 6
  breakdown of, 13

J

Jargon File (The Hacker's Dictionary), 5
Jolitz, William and Lynne, 15

K

Kipling, Rudyard, 164
Kropotkin, Pyotr Alexeyvich, 51

L

license restrictions for software,
  133
licenses (open source), 72
  ownership and, 73
Linus's law, 30
Linux
  category killers and, 93
  for-profit packagers and, 133
  ideology of hacker culture and,
    70
  kernels, early releases of, 29
  open source and, 21
  origins of, 15
  promoting for open source
    movement, 177
  stable and unstable versions,
    32
  World Wide Web and, 17
LISP
  code archives, evolution of, 27
LISP (AI language), 6
Locke, John, 76–79

M

MACRO-10, 5
maintenance, for software, 118
Maslow, Abraham, 83
MATLAB, 28
maximizaing reputation incen-
  tives, 85
Memoirs of a Revolutionist
  (Kropotkin), 51
Microsoft
  Halloween Documents and,
    183
  Internet Explorer, 135, 172
MIME (Multipurpose Internet
  Mail Extensions), 44
Minix, 24
  Andy Tanenbaum and, 43
MIT, 4–6
Motorola 68000 microchip, 11
Mozilla organization, 135, 174
  mismanagement of, 186
Multics, 8
Mythical Man-Month (Brooks),
  25, 32

N

Netscape Communications, Inc.,
  open-sourcing browsers,
    135, 173
Netscape Public License (NPL),
  134
New Hacker's Dictionary, 169
noosphere, definition of, 77
NPL (Netscape Public License),
  134

O

Oh, Seung-Hong (programer), 24
Ohio State Emacs Lisp arcive, 28
open source, 4
  business ecology of, 152
  company competition and,
    148–151

The cover of this book was designed and produced in Adobe Photoshop 5.0 and QuarkXPress 4.1 with Interstate and Sabon fonts. The cover illustration, "Composition with Figures," was painted by Livbov Popova in 1913. It is part of the collection of the State Tetraykov Gallery.

The interior of the book is set in Adobe's Sabon font, which was designed by Jan Tschichold in 1964. The roman design is based on Garamond; the italic is based on typefaces created by Robert Granjon, one of Garamond's contemporaries. Sabon is a registered trademark of Linotype-Hell AG and/or its subsidiaries.

Composition was done using GNU Emacs, the DocBook 4.1 markup language, and a set of formatting tools developed by Steve Talbott, Norm Walsh, and Lenny Muellner using perl and GNU troff.

Many people contributed to this project, including Tim O'Reilly, Edie Freedman, Sarah Jane Shangraw, Claire Cloutier, Lenny Muellner, David Futato, Melanie Wang, Emma Colby, Joe Wizda, Catherine Morris, Emily Quill, Matt Hutchinson, Sue Willing, Betsy Waliszewski, and Mark Brokering.

CPSIA information can be obtained
at www.ICGtesting.com
Printed in the USA
BVOW09s1920200617
487383BV00004B/7/P